DATE DUE

JUN 1 5 1987	DEC 2 9 2012	
SEP 5 1987		
0 7 2 9 9 4		
MAR 1 8 1996		
DEC 0 6 1997		
FEB 0 8 1998		
MAR 1 4 1998		
NOV 0 5 1999		
APR 0 1 2002		
DEC 0 6		

GAYLORD

DOLTON PUBLIC LIBRARY DIST.
849-2385

11-86

PRISON LIFE
IN AMERICA

PRISON LIFE IN AMERICA

BY ANNA KOSOF

A GROLIER COMPANY

FRANKLIN WATTS
NEW YORK ■ LONDON
TORONTO ■ SYDNEY ■ 1984

Dedicated to Del, Tammy, Jo, José,
my family, and especially Stefan

Graph by Vantage Art

Photographs courtesy of:
Bettmann Archive, Inc.: p. 13;
UPI: pp. 18, 21, 35, 54, 75, 84;
Sam Falk from Monkmeyer Press Photo Service: p. 23;
Ethan Hoffman/Archive Pictures, Inc.: p. 28.

Library of Congress Cataloging in Publication Data

Kosof, Anna.
Prison life in America.

Includes index.
Summary: An account of prison life in America today,
both for men and women, emphasizing the dehumanization
of the experience and suggesting alternatives.
1. Prisons—United States—Juvenile literature.
2. Prisoners—United States—Juvenile literature.
[1. Prisons. 2. Prisoners] I. Title.
HV9471.K67 1984   365'.6'0973   84-7340
ISBN 0-531-04860-8

CONTENTS

ACKNOWLEDGMENTS

This book could have never been written without the immense help that so many people graciously offered me.

I am deeply indebted to the 150 or so inmates who shared with me their life stories—events from the past that at times were very painful to recall. My special appreciation goes to Superintendent Frank Headley at Bedford Hills Correctional Facility in New York State. Without his help, I could never have done so much of my research. I would like to thank Commissioner Thomas Couglin and the New York State Department of Corrections for giving me access to the system, with great freedom and few restrictions. Also, my thanks to Assistant Superintendent Carlos Baca and the Colorado State Correctional System for permitting me, in a most generous way, to do research in their facility.

I must also thank Reality House; Project Real; and Fortune Society, especially David Rothenberg, whose insights were invaluable; the New York Urban Coalition, especially José Ferrer and Arthur Barnes. I cannot stress enough that this book could not have been written without their help, their encouragement, their time, and their deep commitment. And I would not be fair if I did not thank my editor, Marjory Kline, who helped shape this book. A personal word of thanks to Diane, Judy, David, and Melvin, who put up with me throughout this process. I of course could not forget Sandra and the women at Fiske.

FOREWORD

Let me begin with a word of advice and caution to the reader, especially the young reader: this book should not be viewed as leisure reading for relaxation. Rather, it is an unsettling, step-by-step guide along a sure path to a dead-end future.

Harsh facts of life have motivated the writing of this book. One is the fact of prison life: who goes there, how one "qualifies," and what happens after admission. The prison population in these United States numbers a staggering half a million people—even discounting all those persons in local jails and other forms of detention. There are more black males of college age, for example, locked up behind bars than enrolled in college. Such tragic truths extract a terrible human toll and an enormous social cost—a waste of life at taxpayers' expense. It costs more to house a prisoner than to send a young person to even the most expensive college or university. Even if the existence of crime makes prisons necessary, a fact of prison life is that it is wasteful and costly.

But that is the end result of the story. Other facts suggest its beginning. Unemployment among the nation's teenagers remains at intolerably high levels. In New York City, for example, fewer than 20 percent of all teenagers (between the ages of sixteen and nineteen) and fewer than 10 percent of black teenagers have either part-time or full-time jobs. Yet independent research has found the high-school dropout rate for eleventh graders at levels of 50 percent for whites, 72 percent for blacks, and 80 percent for Hispanics. On any given school day in New York City, there are more truants on the streets, in the subways, and elsewhere than there are people in the New York State capital of Albany or in any city in West Virginia, Delaware, or Wyoming. A 1981 National Assessment of Educational Progress found that 47 percent of urban black teenagers were functionally illiterate. The path from school to work is so filled with obstacles that it is a route not traveled by increasing numbers of youth.

With insufficient education, no skills, no job, and no income, the temptation of the illegal "fast buck" becomes irresistible to many youths. The lure is most enticing to those most lacking in other earning options. As would be expected given population ratios, more whites are arrested for crimes than blacks; but blacks are over five times more likely to spend time behind bars. And once a person bites at the lure of crime and is caught (and locked up), it is hard to get off the hook.

That's the potentially saving message Anna Kosof so clearly conveys. *Doing* time means *losing* time. Time in prison puts a halt to—not a hold on—the future. A young person who goes to prison is likely to leave there just as unprepared, unskilled, and unemployable as he or she was before. One thing has been acquired—a prison record. A prison record can slam the door on future opportunity. Perhaps that's why prison is often called "the slammer."

But this book will do more than scare the potentially tempted. It will serve also to inform the politically responsible. It is not enough simply to avoid the trap that ensnares others. In a democracy, responsible citizens, together with their chosen public officials, should be politically involved in changing the conditions that lead to crime and altering those factors that make the prison experience a sure ticket to a dead-end future. It means seeking alternatives to prison for some offenders and insisting upon training and rehabilitation for those who do end up there. It also means pursuing policies that increase legitimate income-earning opportunities. Locking people up and forgetting them virtually ensures that they will be forever forgotten.

Read and heed this book; then act accordingly.

H. Carl McCall
Commissioner
New York State
Division of Human Rights

1

WHO IS IN PRISON?

You probably don't know anyone who is in prison, yet prisoners are very much a part of all of our lives. They are in our minds when we spend millions of dollars buying locks for our doors, gates for our windows. They are an influence in our lives when we don't go out at night. Or when your parents worry about your hitchhiking with a stranger. Prisoners are convicted of crimes. They make headlines daily. They take up a good part of the nightly news. Who are these prisoners?

"Who are these prisoners?" John McInnes, an ex-convict, repeated my question. "It's funny that you ask, because in a way it's very easy to figure out who these people are. You can almost predict who will be in prison."

John, now thirty-six years old, looks a lot older than his age. He dropped out of high school before he finished the eleventh grade. At age seventeen, he was smoking marijuana and drinking. The following year he was convicted of stealing from a department store.

"After that year, things just got worse very rapidly. I started holding up people, getting drunk almost every day, and hanging out with experienced criminals. I gave up looking for a job. I didn't even know how to go about it. So I got busted for robbery and spent the next five years in prison."

There are over 400,000 people in prison in America. That figure does not include the nearly 7 million that pass through our jails yearly, or the over 250,000 on parole, or the 1.2 million people on probation.

Today's prison inmates are predominantly poor, young adult males with less than a high-school education. Prison is not a new experience for many of them; they have been incarcerated (imprisoned) before, many for the first time as juveniles. The offense that brought them to prison was usually a violent crime or a property crime such as auto theft or burglary. Many have a history of drug and alcohol abuse.

The lack of education seems to be a key factor. Nearly three out of every five inmates did not complete high school; as a group, they averaged eleven years of schooling. The lack of a high-school diploma undoubtedly contributed to their employment problems and low income prior to the arrest that led to incarceration. Only 60 percent had been working full time. Among the rest of the group, half had given up looking for work. One-fifth of them had no income at all for the twelve months prior to arrest.

As for the racial composition, 50 percent of the prisoners are classified as white, and 48 percent as black (this figure is consistent with those for unemployment and poverty in the black communities across America). The prison population is predominantly male, with about 7 percent females. Young people, from eighteen to twenty-nine years of age, compose the largest group. Less than 1 percent are under eighteen and only 4 percent are over fifty years old. As one of the inmates put it, "By the time you're fifty, you either get some sense or you die." So, when John said to me that you can almost predict who will be in prison, in a way he is right. There is a real pattern to who commits crimes. After all, only 4 percent of the prison population have a college education.

When we think of someone who commits a crime, we create an image in our minds. We imagine this person as capable of doing very cruel things, things that those in their right minds would not do. Therefore, it is not surprising to learn that there is a strong relationship between crime and drug and alcohol abuse. Almost a third of all prisoners were under the influence of an illegal drug when they committed the crimes for which they were imprisoned. More than half had taken drugs during the month just prior to their crimes. The facts are just as strong when it comes to alcohol. Almost a third of all inmates said that they had been drinking heavily just before they committed the offense for which they were convicted. Almost one out of five of the inmates drank heavily every day the entire year before they entered prison. Habitual offenders and persons convicted of assault, burglary, and rape were more likely to be heavy drinkers than other prisoners. Among drug users, 40 percent were heroin addicts, and the others were habitual users of marijuana and other drugs.

Of course, the crimes that we usually hear about are the violent ones. These are the ones that attract media attention and the ones that we most fear. In actual fact, 57 percent of prisoners had been convicted of violent crimes, and that figure is on the rise. Among these offenders, 30 percent had committed murder or manslaughter, and 45 percent robbery. About a third of all inmates were convicted of property crimes, and more than half these were burglaries.

If you are wondering what has changed about the prison population over the years, the most obvious fact is that there has been a continual increase in this population and it is growing to staggering numbers. (Compare today's prison population figure of over 400,000 with that of 90,000 in 1925.) Between 1972 and 1978 the number of persons in our country age eighteen to thirty-four rose 15 percent. According to figures compiled by the U.S. Department of Justice, this is the principal age group from which the incarcerated are drawn. The increase by this age group, far greater than that for the population as a whole, was a major factor in the rise in the number of prison inmates during the 1970s. It is believed that this age group will comprise fewer people during the 1980s and this will have an impact on the huge prison population in the next few years.

If you count the number of people in prison—that is, people who have been convicted—and the number of people in jail—that is, people who are waiting to be tried or sentenced, or are in jail because there is no room for them in prison—and the number of people on probation and parole, today there are well over two million people who are either accused or convicted of committing a crime. That is a larger number than the population of many of our states. And most of the people in trouble with the law are between nineteen and forty years of age—a very high number of whom are younger people. Aside from the tremendous increase in prison population, the crimes are increasingly more violent in nature, and the number of women in prison is on the rise. It is estimated that the prisons are 24–50 percent over capacity, and numerous states are under a court order to reduce dangerous overcrowding of inmates. Obviously, this situation is ripe for disaster.

How does this all begin? First, kids have problems in school and at home. They drop out of school, some of them already having been involved in minor juvenile crimes. They do not have a job; many of them are not even looking for a job anymore. (Among black teenagers, unemployment is over 50 percent.) Without education, without a job, they turn to crime as a way to survive and out of boredom. However, alcohol and drug use is a very significant part of this picture of a typical prisoner. Some of the prisoners that I talked with told me that they could not have committed their crimes without the use of drugs or alcohol. Even worse, often those who were heavily under the influence of alcohol did not really remember what crime they had committed.

Seventy percent of the people who go to prison are repeaters. Not only are they uneducated and unable to get a job, but once they have a prison record, they have a stigma to overcome. They are "criminals," and years of prison life have made them angrier and more frustrated. They are young, many are violent, and they have a distorted vision through the use of alcohol and drugs. They are people that we all fear, and yet they were not always this way. What went wrong, and how could this happen to two million Americans?

2

SHORT HISTORY OF PRISONS

Prison is a relatively recent idea. Sanctions in the ancient world consisted primarily of slavery or indentureship to the victim or the victim's family, employment on public-works projects, mutilation or amputation, banishment, or death. There were no trials or sentences as we think of them today. Certainly, the very concept of long-term confinement as the most common form of punishment is a recent idea. The first court probably appeared around 2000 B.C. for the purposes of settling blood feuds—most commonly, property settlements.

Interestingly, before the concept of "prisons" evolved, temples were used for sanctuary. Places were set aside to which the accused could flee. In those cases where the accused did not manage to find a sanctuary, he or she was punished severely by the accuser; if the crime was serious, death was a common way for settling the issue.

The first actual place built for the purpose of confining prisoners can be traced to the seventh century B.C. The Greeks constructed underground chambers to hold prisoners awaiting trial. Plato, the Greek philosopher, concerned himself with the issue of crime way back in the fifth century B.C. He wrote that there should be three prisons: one in the city for persons awaiting trial and sentence, one for the reform of disorderly persons, and the third, far from the city, for the punishment of felons. In a way, we have the first and the third in the modern-day prison. The place to reform the disorderly, or a place for rehabilitation, seems to be the one that many people argue we still need, or need more of.

Throughout ancient and medieval times, custody for people who committed crimes was dealt with in what is considered private prisons. People who had power and money could build their own prisons and incarcerate those who interfered with their political ambitions. These private prisons were built until about 1800. Crime was not considered to be the state's problem. Many of the disputes were handled between the two parties involved. The practice of dueling, as a solution to private disputes, continued into the European colonization of America.

The transport of serious offenders to a distant land began in England after 1600. England's first law for deportation was passed in 1597. Do you know where these people were sent? Here, to the Americas. When it is said that America was founded by criminals, that's not far from wrong. The British government emptied out its jails and shipped the prisoners over the sea. In the mid-nineteenth century, France and Russia, too, routinely sent their "criminals" to faraway places. Consequently, the need to build prisons for serious offenders was delayed for a while.

It was only after the American Revolution that the

British stopped sending their felons here. Instead, "convict ships" were put into use. These ships were equipped with chains, torture devices, and barbaric equipment to put people to death in particularly gruesome ways. Many of the prisoners died at sea.

The first prison in America was built in 1773 at Simsbury, Connecticut, about fifty miles north of New Haven. The first inmate escaped eighteen days after he was sent there. You can imagine, it lacked adequate security.

In 1815, New York State established a prison at Auburn. This prison provided for confinement of inmates at night in individual cells, a regimen of work during the day, and harsh discipline in general. Since maintaining prisons was beginning to be expensive, the prisoners were rented out for various types of work, the authorities reasoning that in this way the prisoners would help pay for their keep rather than be a burden to the taxpayers. The prisoners performed hard manual labor, such as working on roads and railways. Many of the inmates died from beatings, poor food, and overwork.

The majority of the prisons, other than in the South, were built at a time when large industrial facilities were favored. Today, these huge prisons, usually located in isolated areas, are still in use. Prisons in the Deep South developed in a different way; to begin with, the buildings were smaller. Mississippi, for example, developed large agricultural operations. The

Convicts are shown at hard labor in a Georgia quarry about the year 1919. A guard oversees the work from a watchtower.

function of these prison farms was referred to as "work therapy." In Texas, as well as in some other Southern states, agriculture is still practiced as "work therapy."

Today's prisons and correctional institutions are the products of long-term evolution and development. The United States has one of the largest prison populations in the entire world, as well as the greatest growth in number of prisoners since 1925 when we started compiling these statistics. So that you will have some idea of how the prison population is a reflection of society, let me give you some background on the growth rate. The average yearly growth rate of the population of the United States from 1925 to 1981 was 1.2 percent; for the prison population, it was 2.4 percent (twice the growth rate of the population at large). But the growth rate in the prison population has not been steady since 1925. Between 1925 and 1939 the number of sentenced prisoners grew by 88,000, an average of 5 percent, even though there was virtually no growth in the general population during the depth of the Depression, 1932 to 1934. By 1939, the incarceration rate had reached 137 prisoners for every 100,000 people, a level it was not to reach again for forty-one years. Needless to say, general economic conditions in this country greatly affect the crime rate. Whenever there is a large percentage of people unemployed, there seems to be an increase in illegal activities and lawlessness.

Wars, too, affect the crime rate. During World War II, the prison population declined by nearly 50,000. Because most of the people in prison are men, and are between the ages of eighteen and twenty-nine, the prison population declined when many potential offenders were drafted into the army. During the Vietnam era, between 1961 and 1968, the prison population declined by 30,000. In 1968 the prison population

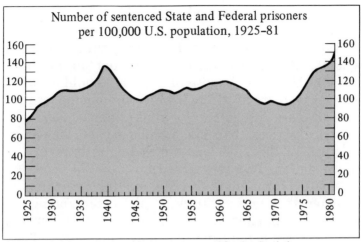

Number of sentenced State and Federal prisoners per 100,000 U.S. population, 1925–81

Source: U.S. Department of Justice, Bureau of Justice Statistics

was 188,000, the lowest since the late 1920s. From this low rate, it grew rather slowly for the next five years. In 1974 it began a dramatic rise that resulted in the addition of nearly 150,000 inmates. By 1982, the incarceration rate was the highest ever recorded.

By now you might have the idea that prisons as we know them today are a relatively new concept, and that the number of people we have in prison and the rate of growth are a major problem. Remembering the numbers is not very important, but it is important that you do understand that statistical changes in the prison population are a direct reflection of what is occurring outside the prison walls. Wars affect the prison population. The number of young men in a society has a real impact on the rise in prison population. (A so-called "baby boom," when an unusually large number of people have children, will eventually result in an increase in the number of people who are incarcerated when that generation turns about eighteen.) Bad economic conditions and high unemployment have a great impact on the prison population.

With this bit of history, let us turn our attention to what it is like to be in prison. We are not talking about being in jail. The purpose of a jail is to hold accused persons who are awaiting trials or sentencing, or persons who are convicted of a minor offense, usually a sentence of less than six months—a misdemeanor. Jails are in the city, sometimes in the back of the police station. Theoretically, people are not supposed to be jailed for more than a few months, regardless of whether they are awaiting trial or sentencing. In prison, the inmates have been convicted, sentenced, and have a specific time that they must serve. They are convicts.

To enter a prison door is one of the most dramatic things that can happen to you. Fear sets in just at the sight of the barbed-wire gate and doors that seem so permanently shut. The first time I went into a prison, I was scared, even though I knew that I could leave. But what if there is a fire and I get trapped behind those locked, steel bars? I asked myself. "Will the guards really let me out? What if someone makes a mistake? What if I can't get out? Is there a phone inside? Will I be cut off from the outside world?" Can you imagine yourself going to prison, knowing that it will be your home for the next five or ten years? It is scary. You feel really helpless, with no control of your life. You can't sleep or eat when you want to; you can't walk around or take a shower when you want to. Prison really means living without freedom. Let's take a closer look at life in prison.

3

MEN IN PRISON

"The worst thing about being in prison is that you can't sleep. You hear the keys clinking, the cell doors opening, people shouting, the guards screaming—all night long."

That is a common complaint from inmates. After spending several hours in a prison, I began to be disturbed by the noise level. I should mention that most prisons are built of cement—sounds are magnified, echoing from ceilings, walls, and floors. The opening and closing of the gates are endless. There are gates almost every few feet, and someone has to unlock and relock every individual gate, so the sound of keys is a part of the daily noise of prison life.

Prisons can be very different from one another. Some look like what we have seen in the movies. They have tremendous stone walls and a watchtower that provides a view of the buildings and prison yards. Many of the minimum-security facilities are located

The bloodiest riot in American prison history
took place at the New Mexico State Penitentiary at
Santa Fe in 1980. This photograph is of the control
center a year after the riot. Notice the "count"
board in the background and the key rack to the left.

in the cities and look like any institutional building; you would not know from the outside that they are prisons. Then, too, there are more modern facilities that are located in rural areas. Some of them, only one story aboveground, with underground chambers, have no gates at all, but have a master control room full of buttons that control the opening and closing of all doors. Many of the prisons have long hallways, and the cell blocks are separated into different buildings, with a recreational area and sometimes a large mess hall that serves that area. Usually, if an inmate is in a cell block, much of his activity will take place in that cell block, except when he goes to school, or work, or for medical treatment.

The cells are very small, with a bed, dresser, toilet, and sink, and perhaps a plant. Because of the tremendous overcrowding that exists in most prisons, some of them house two people in one cell. On the other hand, some of the minimum-security facilities have a dormitory-style area with no cells at all, or are composed of small rooms with doors that the inmates can close or even lock. They look a little like any small college dormitory.

Just as prisons are not all alike, the prison experience and what prisoners do all day varies. Perhaps what is a common thread, though, is that all prisoners are without their freedom, without the ability to make decisions about their movements and that they have a lot of time to themselves. A lot of time to think and be alone in a little room.

The prison day begins very early in the morning. In most places, the morning starts with a "count." A count is the procedure by which the prisoners are accounted for. That can be done either as a head count, with the prisoner in his cell or outside his cell, or a hand count, with the inmate putting his hand through the cell bars for the count. In a maximum-security prison, there may be a count every two to four hours. In fact, sometimes it seems as if inmates are being counted all day long.

Feeding the inmates can take at least an hour or more. A prison guard (or, as others call them, "officer") asked that I not use the word "feeding" because it makes peole think of a zoo, with animals being fed. But it really looks that way. All the inmates from one cell block are marched to the mess hall in single file and escorted through the food line. After getting their food in cafeteria style, they sit in a designated order. After they finish eating (and usually complaining about the food that they have eaten), they are taken back to their cells. Usually, it's still very early, six-thirty or seven in the morning. That's the way the day begins, the same day that will repeat itself perhaps for years, with little or no variation.

Then come the assignments. Most of the inmates do something, or they are supposed to do something. They either go to school or work in the prison or work in what is known as prison industry. School can mean getting a high-school diploma or taking college courses or even getting a college degree. Because most of the prison population do not have a high-school diploma, many inmates take advantage of the opportunity to receive an education. While there are not enough jobs to go around, many prisoners make a few dollars a week working in the prison. (About three-fourths of the states pay something.) The pay scale may range from a nickel up to a dollar a day. That can add up to about twenty dollars a month. The work assignments are determined by various considerations, including behavior, the length of the prison sentence, the prisoner's classification, general attitude, and performance.

A prison is a huge community. Greenhaven, for example, located in Stormville, New York, houses

**This factorylike complex is Greenhaven,
located in Stormville, New York.**

over two thousand people. That entails providing three meals a day, changing two thousand sheets on the beds once a week, a tremendous amount of clerical work (some of which is done by the inmates) cutting a large area of grass, cleaning the floors that two thousand people walk on, doing the dishes, and so on. A prison is really like a small autonomous town, requiring all the services that any town must have.

There is a category called "prison industry" where prisoners make a product that the prison sells to the state, like license plates, or provide a service such as maintaining forests or roads and public recreational facilities.

After a few hours of either work, school, or training, the prisoners are escorted back to their cells for another count. Usually before lunch they go through an hour of "count" again. Now, you may wonder, why a count is so important. At every correctional facility, they consider security to be the most important function. "You cannot have good programs in a place where there is no good security," a deputy superintendent, director of programs, said to me. At all times they must know where every inmate is supposed to be, and he better be there or the "count" could not add up correctly. When the count doesn't check out, prison routine comes to a halt until it does. One day I waited in one cell block for almost an hour to be taken over to the next cell block because all the correctional officers were busy with the count. Obviously, if a prisoner escapes, it will take very little time before it becomes apparent that he is missing.

**Prisoners watch
television in a cell
block at San Quentin.**

The afternoons are very much like the mornings. Some of the facilities have drug- or alcohol-treatment programs, or arts and craft programs; sometimes the inmates go back to work or have visitors. By four o'clock they are back in their cells. Of course, there is a count; then comes dinner. At night, aside from watching television or writing or reading, there is not a lot to do. Each floor usually has at least one television set (and fights often break out over which channel to turn on), and there is a recreational area where the inmates can play cards and other games. By nine o'clock at night, they are locked in their individual cells.

That is what life is like at some of the facilities, but minimum-security prisons are very different. The security is relaxed, the buildings are much smaller and less institutionalized, and the tension is lower. The counts are fewer. You don't see prisoners marched down the halls; you don't have to wait for a guard to unlock gates every few feet. But then, as mentioned before, minimum-security facilities are either for people who have committed less serious crimes or are serving the last stretch of a long sentence that began at a maximum-security facility. Usually these places are a little quieter, without the familiar sound of the keys.

After I spent some days in prison, inmates always asked me if I could really feel as though I were in prison. "No," I said. "I know that I am leaving at the end of the day and will not be locked inside a cell that is as big as most people's bathroom." But even though no one can really experience the feeling of being in prison unless they are incarcerated, when you walk past some of the gates and the doors lock behind you, you really do feel the sense of being captive to someone else, you feel powerless and realize that you are trusting your life in someone else's hands. Every time they closed the gates behind me, I thought of what would happen if there was a fire. I thought about the toilet overflowing next to the bed. The loss of total privacy is very obvious. Your cell is open for all the guards to see. You cannot even urinate without doing it in public. You cannot lie in bed in the nude on a hot summer night, and those cells can be extremely hot during the summer.

I asked Charles what bothered him the most about being in prison.

"Your loss of humanity, the loneliness, and having no control over your life," he said.

I wondered why it was so lonely—after all, the inmates are always in large groups.

Charles replied, "That's why. You are always with hundreds of people. You are told every moment where to go, what to do. People are screaming all day, and you can't have a private conversation without twenty guys being there. Then you are alone from nine o'clock at night till the next morning. Sometimes you don't want to read and it takes time to get used to sleeping here."

Prisons can also be very frightening, so that in both male and female facilities, inmates tend to form groups for mutual protection. I mentioned to an inmate that I was surprised that the men were in such great physical shape.

"You have to be," was his answer. "If you are not, and if you don't have a group to protect you, you can get killed in here."

Fights and rapes and even murders are not uncommon in prisons. Fights are a daily occurrence, while rapes and murders are reported less frequently. Men at one of the prison facilities told me that homosexual activity is very common. Some of the fights have to do with sexual activities, but almost anything could cause an argument. "After all, you have two thousand men locked in here. Some have been here for five or ten years; they are angry; they are tense; and some of them are also murderers. You know everybody in here is not an angel." The man who made that statement was in prison for armed robbery, but he didn't think of himself as dangerous.

Groups are formed usually along racial lines. The blacks, the whites, and the Hispanics stay within their own group. Some individual friendships are formed, but it is the group that protects them. All the prisoners I talked with agreed that it was the only way to survive in prison.

"What do the guards do?" I asked.

"What can a guard do? Sometimes they are by themselves and ten guys are about to get into a fight. Besides, they never know what started the fight. Sometimes a cigarette can start a fight. You have a whole system of merchants in here. People are buying and selling everything from drugs to sex to you name it."

I asked the prison officials about these activities, and they acknowledged that some of that certainly does go on in prison, but they were convinced that not all of the inmates are involved.

I really couldn't figure out how the drugs got in there, since anyone who visits a prison is screened. Bags are searched and sometimes even the visitors' shoes. And, too, each inmate is supposed to be completely searched after each visit. It was pointed out to me, however, that even with all those precautions, it is possible for visitors to smuggle drugs into inmates.

"Let's face it, these guys have all day long to cook up schemes as to how they are going to do something. They also have had a few years on the streets of sneaking in and out of people's homes and stores, stealing, and, of course, buying drugs and not getting arrested. If a drug addict was arrested every time he bought drugs, he would be arrested daily, even twice daily."

The most exciting thing that can happen to an inmate is a visit from his family. In New York State, as well as several other states, the family can visit an inmate every day from nine o'clock in the morning until three o'clock in the afternoon and all day Saturday. Visitation is limited to family members, lawyers or the clergy, or a common-law wife. All visitors must have prior approval from the prison officials.

Perhaps one of the main concerns that any inmate has is where he will serve his sentence. Most of the maximum-security facilities tend to be very far from the city, making visits from the family very difficult because of the long trip and the expense that the family would have to endure. When I visited Sing Sing, one of the oldest and best-known correctional facilities, at Ossining, New York, I traveled on a train full of women and children and lots of packages—packages for the inmates. Most of the people who get off the train at Ossining are going to visit a family member in Sing Sing. From the train station, for one dollar, a car will take you to the prison, which is up the hill from the station. Because it was a weekday there were far fewer visitors than there would be on a weekend, when two hundred or three hundred people might visit the prison.

Upon arrival, the women have to go through security. Their purses are searched, and they are checked with a metal detector. The packages they brought with them are turned over to the guards. A visitor is not supposed to either give or receive anything from an inmate directly without staff approval. Any money brought to an inmate for commissary goods must be given to an officer, who keeps a record of the inmate's account. The women place their pocketbooks in lock-

A prison visiting room

ers and then they enter a large room with long tables and benches where they wait while the inmates are located and as a group brought down from each cell block. This is considered a private visit, or a face-to-face visit. If an inmate isn't attending classes or at work, he can talk to his family until visiting hours are up, when he must leave and return to his cell.

"I don't know, I think that the visits are the hardest to take sometimes. I look forward to seeing my family all week; then they come, and I feel terrible. You can't talk to your wife or kids in a room with hundreds of other people. It's so noisy in there, you can't even hear yourself," Charles complained, as Art, who served three years in Attica, listened.

"I was in the middle of nowhere for three years, with two visits the entire time, and I would have given a lot to have visits like this. It may not be like sitting in your living room, but I tell you, it is very, very lonely to be so far away without any outside visits. That's real punishment. In fact, I think that that is the punishment. Isolation. I finally served the last part of my sentence close to New York City, and it has made a big difference to me. My old lady comes regularly, brings food, and I get to see my daughter. I feel a hell of a lot better. I have something to look forward to."

Like Art's common-law wife, about 80 percent of the women remain loyal to their men while they are in prison. The women are allowed to bring all sorts of foods, and a lot of them bring enough food so that some inmates eat only one meal a day in the mess hall.

"How did your daughter feel about seeing you in here?" I asked Charles.

"She thinks that I am in a hospital. Also, I don't want my wife to bring her too much. She asks too many questions and gets very restless. But she's only four, so there's no need to tell her where I am really at.

She thinks that I am really very sick and wonders when I will ever get out."

Art disagreed with that approach. "My kid knows where I am. I want my daughter to know that if you do something wrong you have to pay the price. I want her to be afraid. She doesn't come too much either because it is too hard on everybody, but I do see her about once a month, now that I'm closer to the city."

Before the problem of overcrowding, one of the methods of punishing an inmate who misbehaved was to send him farther and farther away from the city he came from, so that he would have fewer visits.

It's a little different for women. Most of the men in their lives leave the women once they go to prison. About 20 percent of the men continue to visit them, but their mothers and their children come regularly if they are not too far from the city. At female facilities, you see the difference in who comes to see them. At Bedford Hills Correctional Facility, there is a Sesame Street–type room where a mother can really play with her visiting children, rather than just having them sit and get restless and bored.

I came back on the train from Sing Sing with the family of one of the inmates, and I could see that it really took a toll on them. The inmate's wife told me that she visits him regularly, at least once a week. She feels that that's the only way to ensure that they will have a relationship when he gets out. Now that he is in prison, they are getting along well, but before he was imprisoned he was involved with the "street life" and she hardly ever saw him. She believes that when he gets out this time he'll stay straight and get a job. While on the train her two children never stopped asking about their father.

"What did he really do wrong? You said he'll be out soon. When is he really coming out? Why are those policemen always standing there in that room with a gun? I want to see the room that my daddy lives in. Why can't I see his room?"

Paula, their mother, answered the questions as patiently as she could, then she almost begged them to stop. "Listen, I have answered your questions before, now leave me alone." The children were obviously a little shaken by the trip, but Paula said that they are always like that after a visit. Still, she feels that it is important that they see their father.

It was Paula's husband who said to me that after each visit he decides that he will never come back to prison.

"After they leave is when I feel that I have been really punished. I was a lousy father when I was on the streets. I hardly ever saw them, and never played with them. But having them see me like this really makes me think about what I am doing. They see you like a boy, ordered around by a guard, feeling so unlike a man. I know I got a good family, and I really can't do this to them anymore. I want to be with them. I want to be a father to those kids before it is all over. They feel pain every time they go to school and the other kids tease them about their daddy being a jailbird. That's the reason that I am not going to commit crimes."

It's very emotional for everyone, but, then again, ten years ago in most states, an inmate could only talk to his family by phone through a glass booth. Certainly, feeling the closeness and being able to touch your family is a lot better than the old days when visits like that were unheard of.

Not only can inmates see their families daily, but seven states have what is known as "conjugal" or trailer visits. That means that once in a while an inmate can spend a weekend alone in a trailer with his wife and children. Although the trailer is on prison grounds, guards are not there to monitor the visit. Trailer visits represent a major change in the prison system.

These visits are both wonderful and very depressing for both the inmates and their families. For the inmates, because these visits are rare, it is something to look forward to and keeps them on good behavior, since only the best-behaved inmates can take part in these visits. It is a way to be alone with their families. But I talked with a few inmates the day after they had spent a weekend with their families, and the reality of separation had set in.

"After a trailer visit, I can be more resolved than ever not to come back here. I can't stand to see them leave, to know the pain that I have caused my family," said one of the men.

Perhaps the trailer visits are real rehabilitative tools. If the inmates feel that way, maybe they will really try to stay out of prison. However, those who were able to get trailer visits admitted that they also looked forward to the visits because they were able to get away from the mess hall, their cells, the guards, and the noise. "It was like going on a brief vacation."

4

WOMEN IN PRISON

Prisons for women are as different from male facilities as being in a football locker room is from a ballet class. The most obvious difference is on the walls. Where it is permitted, the men have pictures of naked ladies in all positions tacked on their walls and the women have pictures of their children on their walls. As a guard who worked at both male and female facilities put it, "Male prisons smell like men, while female facilities smell like perfume."

The first apparent difference is the physical setting. Some of the maximum male prisons house as many as two thousand people, which in itself produces a tremendous sense of tension. Just the noise level, the constant fear of incidents, the fights, and the size of the men create a feeling—a feeling of fear. The security is even different. In a women's prison, although all the cells are locked, the guards are still in uniform, and the place still looks like an institution, it feels—for lack of a better way to describe it—more genteel and more feminine. I don't want to give you the idea that women wear nightgowns and pink dresses; they wear prison uniforms just like men do. In most states green seems to be the preferred color for prison garb. The prisoners wear green pants or skirts and white shirts, with black or brown flat shoes. But it is not just the physical place that seems different, it is the population who's in there.

Women still make up less than 10 percent of the prison population in America. In a sense, that means that prisons and prison rules are totally geared toward men. Not considered were the realities: women give birth in prison, women have to breast-feed their babies, women go to prison and their children have to be cared for, or that most of the women don't pose the same security problems that men do. They usually don't take hostages, and most of the riots are in male prisons.

In a way, prisons for female offenders seem a little more humane. When you enter any prison, as I noted before, your bag is searched and a metal detector is used to see if you are bringing a gun, or other weapons. But in the female prisons, the guards, most of whom are men, seem to be a little more relaxed about this process. They search visitors but they don't seem to watch as closely as they do in a male facility. Of course, that may be because of my gender.

Bedford Hills Correctional Facility is located in a pleasant setting of trees and grass in a suburban area of New York State. It's a quiet place. Except for its very tall barbed-wire fence, it looks as if it could be a school. Once you see the fence, you probably would guess that it is a prison or a military outpost. It lacks the thick walls that characterize Greenhaven, along with similar prisons built in the last century. The high walls and the isolation must have been a major deter-

A prisoner plays with her baby at the Florida
Correctional Institution for Women at Lowell, Florida.

rent to escape in those days. Even the cell blocks look a little better at Bedford. There are large buildings, with maybe fifty or sixty cells to a floor, whereas at Sing Sing, the cells are arranged in tiers, one on top of another, all facing an open area. It reminded me of a zoo. These don't have windows, though many facilities do have windows. At Sing Sing, too, the cells are separated from each other by walls, but an inmate can yell at other prisoners above him or below him, because of the way the cells are stacked. The long corridor just echoes with the sounds of the entire unit.

"There is nothing worse than being a woman, a drug addict, and being in prison," declared Joan. "Nothing. Your old man leaves you; society gives up on you; your children are embarrassed. Women are not supposed to commit crimes. They are supposed to be home raising children."

That's a point of view that is expressed frequently. Although only a small number of women are in prison compared with the number of men, the figure has grown a lot over the past ten years. There are all types of women in prison. There are women who are poor, who committed drug-related crimes, and then there is a woman like Jean Harris at Bedford Hills, who was convicted of shooting her longtime boyfriend, who came from a privileged background, who is educated, and who was once the headmistress of a girls' finishing school. Some of the women are there for embezzlement of money, a few for robbery, some for homicide or manslaughter, and many for crimes that have to do with supporting drug habits.

Barbara is in prison for the first time. She does not come from a background that seems to produce most of the people in prison—a background of no skills, no education, and welfare. She comes from the middle class. But at some point she lost interest in school and started hanging out with people who were into drugs.

She became a barmaid and started drinking while still using drugs. In her own words, she was headed NOWHERE.

"If I was out on the streets today, I think that I might be dead."

She was lost. Her marriage collapsed. She had a small child who was being cared for by her family. Then, too, she became "gay." She lived with a woman, and when the relationship ended, bitterly, she and a new lover arranged for the woman to be killed.

"Why?"

"She started messing around with my younger sister. My family kept telling me to keep this woman away from my sister. I didn't want my sister to be gay, so after I kept telling her to stay away from my sister and she didn't, I just thought that I had to get rid of her."

Both Barbara and her friend are serving time in a maximum facility for manslaughter.

Barbara is not typical, though most of the women who are in for murder or manslaughter seem to have known their victims. Barbara has pictures of her son on her dresser, and she maintains a closeness with her family. She says that she is not gay anymore, that it was a phase she was going through. She talks a lot about her son and her desire to improve their relationship. Her son, having known the woman who was killed, kept wondering why and how you could kill someone you loved.

"How do you answer that?" I asked.

"You really can't," was her answer. She has relived that nightmare more than once. She still wakes up hearing those shots.

"What do you want to do when you get out?"

"I just want to finish raising my son."

Jane didn't seem to be typical of most women in prison either. She has a soft-looking face and blond hair. She likes to knit. The years have taken their toll on her. She is still attractive, but I suspect that when she came to prison eight years ago, she was a very pretty woman. She is in prison for selling two ounces of cocaine to an undercover agent. She is serving fifteen years, a harsher sentence than some people receive for first-degree murder.

She was not a drug dealer, she contends; she had no record of being an addict. She was a hairdresser with a shop. Why was she carrying the drugs? She says that she was entrapped. Someone she believed to be a friend asked her to see if she could get some cocaine for his cousin. When she did get the cocaine and delivered it, the "cousin" turned out to be an undercover agent. Jane's story seemed plausible. She handled the situation in a way that a sophisticated dealer would never do. She turned over drugs to someone she had never even met before. Usually, experienced drug dealers would drop the drugs on the street; they would not just stand there with cocaine in their possession. Only an amateur would do that. Jane is in her mid-thirties now, and her life will never be the same.

When she was arrested, her entire world shattered. Her boyfriend left her; she has no family. She never thought that she would receive such a harsh sentence for what she considers a mistake. She is a model prisoner. (Those who serve long sentences tend to be the best prisoners. They make a home in prison. They know that they'll be there for a very long time.)

Jane is a very friendly woman, who is waiting for the governor to commute her sentence to a shorter time. She says that all she wants to do is get out of prison and go back to being a hairdresser. If you saw her, in no way would she look like your idea of the tough criminal. Being in prison rather than on the streets makes many of these women look healthier. Although they have a tendency to gain weight from lack of exercise and a high-starch diet, they don't look the same as they did on the streets. Cut off from alcohol and drugs, they have unclouded eyes and healthier skin.

Sandra was more of what is considered a "typical inmate." She was a drug addict with two children. She had been introduced to drugs by her husband and she supported her habit by robbing people daily. I met her a year after she was released from prison. For Sandra and for most of the women, there is a problem of self-image.

"A man can go to prison, come back out, dust himself off, get a job, get a new set of clothes, and be almost like new. A woman can never do that. In this society, the lowest person alive is a Puerto Rican woman who was a junkie, who went to prison. People look at you as if they would like to spit on you. Your children can forgive their father going to prison and committing a crime, but not their mother. My children's father is still serving time upstate. My children still ask about how I could have been a junkie. They sort of accept that from their father." Sandra expressed the feelings of a lot of women.

Women in prison talk mostly about two things: they talk about their children, and they talk about how they feel about being a "fallen woman," being a woman with a prison record, a woman who knows that her children are living through hell while she is in prison. They have a good deal of guilt about that. They cry a lot.

Men in prison are different. They really don't talk too much about their children. Some of them saw very little of their children before they went to prison, so not seeing them while in prison has little effect on them or their children. They talk a lot about politics;

often they blame their crime on society. This is particularly true of the inmates who come from minority backgrounds or poor families. They feel that society denied them a lot of things—a good education, a decent job, adequate housing—so that in order to survive they had to resort to crime. This kind of talk is not heard too much in a women's prison. The women who admit their crime tend to blame themselves rather than anybody else. Usually they feel guilty and want to make amends to their children, even though they realize that by the time they get out, their children will be grown. Sandra, like a lot of women, has managed to stay out of prison and off drugs since she was released. Women seem to have a much lower recidivism (a tendency to return to a criminal behavior pattern) rate than do men. Women tend not to be "career criminals." They either commit onetime violent crimes like homicide, or are on drugs. Of course, drug addicts do commit an endless number of crimes, and are in and out of prison for years while they are on drugs. Many of the women got involved in a life of crime through the influence of their husbands or boyfriends. Many of them had children out of wedlock and at an early age. Many of them drank a lot or used drugs. Some of them convey a sense of failure. Every time they were overwhelmed with problems, every time they got hurt or couldn't pay their rent, they got further into alcohol and drugs. Some of them knew that they were involved in a criminal life style and never had the strength to get out, or they were never sober long enough even to realize how mixed up their lives really were. Without question, most of these women caused an immense amount of pain and hardship for their children. They could not deal with their own lives and in no way could they deal with their children's. They made little effort to provide for their children a secure environment or a consistent life.

Their children had discipline problems in school, and grew up either by themselves or under the care of older brothers or sisters. Mother just wasn't there every day at three o'clock when they came home from school.

Just as some men's prisons do, some women's prisons have provisions for trailer visits, whereby an inmate can spend a weekend with her children alone, or with her entire family. They sleep in the trailer, they eat together, and have a "normal" weekend together. These trailers are on the prison grounds, but at least the women are out of their cells and away from the rest of the inmates. Some of the women try to use these trailer visits to really mend their relationship with their children. They spend time with them, talk to them, and try to help ease the pain of separation. After these visits, the women seem very tired—it is a real reminder of what they have given up. Often they are torn between wanting to spend two days with their family and knowing that the separation afterward will be painful.

Bedford Hills Correctional Facility has a unique program, whereby local residents take some of the children into their homes for the summer so that they can visit their mothers every day. These substitute parents are responsible for taking the children to the prison and bringing them home again, something of an escort and foster-parenting arrangement.

"I spent more time with my kids in prison in a healthy way than I ever did outside," said one of the inmates. "Before, I never spent time really talking to them or playing with them; I was high most of the time. So now, when they come up, we talk, we play games together. It's really sad that I had to wait till I got locked up to be a mother. I feel really bad about that."

Of course, while the mothers may feel bad about

what they did in the past and may really try to change their relationship with their children, in some cases it is too late.

I talked with two children, ages ten and thirteen, whose mother was in prison. They live with their grandmother, who takes care of them. Their grandmother visits their mother, but the children don't want to see her. They are angry and bitter. They feel that their mother neglected them before, and they are not ready to forgive the past.

"Wouldn't it be good for all of you to take this time to see if you can develop a relationship again?" I asked them.

They just shook their heads and said that they'll wait till she gets out of prison and if she is really serious about wanting to be a mother, they can try it then. They no longer seemed to care, but I suspect that they were both so hurt that they wanted to punish their mother for what she had done to them.

Little John said, "Hey, I never saw much of her before, so I really don't miss her now. I just hope that she can get her act together. You know, this is not the first time that she's been locked up. So we're used to not having her around. My grandmother is my mother. When she comes out this time, and if she really changes, then maybe she can be my mother."

Janie said, "You know, it's really great to go to school, and have the kids tease you about your mother being a jailbird. So why should we go up and see her? She shouldn't be there in the first place."

It was interesting to listen to these children, because when I listened to the women, they seemed really to want to be good mothers, now that they weren't able to be with their children. It seemed so sad, particularly because some of these children grow up to be angry and violent and will repeat the pattern of their mother. They will become the next generation of people going to prison. The cycle is almost predictable. The children drop out of school, they have no place to go but the streets, they can't get a job, they get into drugs or alcohol, and before long they are candidates for prison.

Then there are women from middle-class backgrounds who committed "white-collar" crimes, such as embezzlement. Once, Sue had a husband and two children, a house, and a job, and lived very much the typical suburban life. The style of living that she and her family maintained required a good deal of money. Her children had expensive clothes and went to expensive schools. When her marriage collapsed, she was faced with the problem of continuing to enjoy a high standard of living on a reduced income. She worked in a firm where she had access to a computer. Using the computer, she embezzled large sums of money from the company. She was caught and sentenced to three years for that crime. While in prison she has had time to think about her problems, and she realizes that she simply cannot live the same life that she had lived before. Her children would have been better off with fewer pairs of sneakers than to see their mother in prison. She, for one, still maintains a close relationship with them, and her mother comes regularly to visit.

"Didn't you think that it was wrong to steal from your company?"

She never seemed to think that it was so wrong to steal, but she was really sorry that she got caught. She is one of those women who probably will not come back to prison, if for no other reason than the fact that she probably will not be in a position again to embezzle money.

Women in prison are as different from one another as are women in the outside world. Some are tough and rough, some are violent, some are drug addicts, some have killed, and some are women who got into trouble because they were gullible and stupid. Some are in prison because they are protecting their husbands. Some are deeply hurt, some really want to start a new life, and some will continue to do the same thing over and over again. However, most of them have children, and they do talk about them a lot. Some have given birth in prison. Some just want to live a quiet life once they get out. The experience seems to hurt them more than it does men; after all, prison life is sort of a macho experience for some men who live the street life. There is nothing feminine about prison.

While in prison, women form some strong bonds. They become very close to one another. They seem to have a sense of community. Some of them call each other "Ma" and "Pa." Instead of having gangs like the men have, they have "families." Some of the women certainly show a lot of care and concern for one another. While rape in male prisons is common, no one that I talked with in a female prison claimed to have been raped. They do get into stupid little fights, they do scream and yell at one another, but they also turn to each other for love and support. Some of them feel that the outside world has given up on them, so they only have one another.

"How would you feel if your mother was in prison?" asked John, the ten-year-old who would not visit his mother in prison. "I come home every day, feeling that she should be home taking care of me. Instead, she's locked up someplace, behind bars. I feel that it's bad enough for me to be without a mother. I don't want to now go see her crying and then have to leave her after a couple of hours. She shouldn't be there in the first place."

He never seemed to express the same resentment toward his father, a man whom he really didn't know well and who was also an inmate. He did say that it was one thing for a man to be locked up, but women should not do anything that would result in imprisonment.

"My grandmother takes care of us, and she never did nothing wrong, so why couldn't my mother be the same way? She didn't have to do that."

I wondered if John developed these views by himself or if his grandmother also felt this way.

"We never talk about my mother. We don't want to hear about her being in prison. So my grandmother never says nothing bad about her. We feel this way. You say that it's hard on the women. Well, it's hard on us, too. My teacher says she wants to talk to my mother. What am I going to say? 'You can talk to her in the "joint"?' No, I say, 'She ain't here.' But my grandmother is too old to go to school and stuff, so when my teacher asks why no one showed up to a teacher-parent meeting, I just have to lie. It's been pretty hard on us. They say that maybe I'll understand when I get older about my mother. Maybe. That's all that I can say. But I really don't understand her now."

John's mother is in for homicide and will not be out for another ten years. John will be twenty years old then.

5

FISKE COTTAGE: AN ALTERNATIVE WOMEN'S PRISON

Fiske Cottage, located within the Bedford Hills Correctional Facility, houses some twenty-six female inmates. The Fiske Experimental Program was initiated in December, 1982. It is important because in many ways it symbolizes the problems that the prison system is facing on several levels. The most important point about Fiske is that it is a system where the prisoners govern themselves without cells, without being locked in, without bars, without being awakened by guards, and it is a small unit that houses some of the most serious violent offenders.

The "Fiske Women," as some call them, are considered model prisoners chosen from the general prison population. Acceptance into the program is based on a prisoner's motivation, attitude, the length of her sentence, and her behavior. A remarkable fact about the Fiske women is that most of them are in prison for much more than minor offenses: twenty of the twenty-six women are classified as "serious violent offenders." Most of the women are older (between twenty-six and thirty-five years of age), and the sentences are long. Sixty-one percent of the women are serving more than twenty years.

Fiske is totally different from the typical prison. It is a bit like a halfway house, a bit like a college dormitory. Here the women make their own rules concerning their facility. They also set their own goals in regard to work, education, and vocational development. They function as a family, living together without the constant supervision of prison guards.

There is a living room with a television set and a phone room, where they can make collect calls to their families anytime. This in itself is a major departure from most prisons, where inmates can make only one phone call a week, for a maximum of three minutes, with a guard monitoring and timing the call. At Fiske, they can call collect as often as they like. Since it's a collect call, the women are sensitive to the cost factor, and restrict their calls on their own. They do not have a toilet in their room like the rest of the facility, but they share a large dormitory-style bathroom. As for security, the "counts" that are such a major part of prison life are done without locking the prisoners in cells, though counts are taken just as in the other sections of the prison. In the community kitchen, the women prepare their own food. They handle knives and other sharp instruments, something that is not permitted in the usual prison. They have a dining room where they eat together.

What is also fascinating about these women is their relationship with the prison superintendent. In most prisons, a prisoner cannot even tell you who the superintendent is. Here, Superintendent Frank Headley sometimes eats with the Fiske women, plays backgammon with them, spends many evenings talking with them, and uses them as a liaison between the administration and the rest of the inmate population of some five hundred. They are truly role models for the other women as they set an example of self-government and a creative approach to prison life.

"Is this still prison?" I asked some of the women.

"Oh, yes. This is prison. I am going to be here for years."

"I am denied the opportunity to see my children grow up."

"I still can't leave at night."

"I don't have my freedom."

"Oh, it is still very much prison."

Talking to Superintendent Headley, I asked about the cost, which is one of the main concerns about prisons. He told me that the building costs $26,000 rather than the millions that it costs for large prison blocks, but more important, the cost of the Fiske Program is much cheaper than the cost of maintaining the general prison population.

"Why?"

"Well, you don't need the same level of security. You don't need as many guards or as much supervision. They cook their own food, and they don't need to be taken in and out of cells all day long. That's a lot of manpower."

In a way, Fiske symbolizes the main problem that the prison system is facing today. Prisons are extremely expensive. According to the New York State Department of Correction, it costs $26,000 a year to keep someone in prison. It costs millions to build new prisons. Overcrowding is so serious that the state of Illinois, among several other states, has been releasing prisoners for good behavior three to eleven months ahead of their minimum sentence because there is no room for them. Many prisons are under court order not to accept any more inmates because they would be violating the law by double-bunking inmates in a cell that can barely house one person. In California, the authorities are about to put them into tents. Every state has shown a tremendous increase in prison population, with California, Florida, and Texas leading the way with an 18 percent population growth. The only state that showed a decline was Michigan, and that was attributed to a Michigan law that reduces sentences whenever the prison population exceeds capacity.

As with everything else, money is a key factor. Plans for 100,000 new prison beds are on drawing boards across the country, at an estimated cost of $70 billion (not considering inflation) in the next thirty years. What that means is that instead of new schools, libraries, and playgrounds, we are going to build prisons. It means more taxes. It means, too, that we cannot give our youth the things that they need, like up-to-date laboratory equipment, classroom computers, and new textbooks, if all our money is going toward building prisons. Of all the world's nations, only the Soviet Union and South Africa have higher percentages of people locked up.

I had dinner with the women at Fiske. Although the meat sauce was a bit salty, the spaghetti was as good as any restaurant fare. The iced tea could have been better, but, compared with the usual prison food, it was delicious. What disturbed me about these women is that I really didn't think of them as women who had committed terrible crimes. They seemed more like any group of women—having dinner, watching television, cleaning the table, washing dishes, and knitting. One woman was making curtains, cutting fabric with a large pair of scissors.

How could I sit with a group of women talking

about some really frightening crimes and in no way feel danger, no way feel that they were a danger to society? Have they changed that much? I wondered.

"No, it's not that they have changed that much. They have been in prison for a long time, but being in the Fiske environment, where they are treated like human beings, makes them want to act like human beings. Also, these women are really some of the best prisoners around. They are carefully picked; they are longtimers; some have served five or ten years before coming to Fiske; now they are truly trying to put all that behind them and really think about the rest of their life," Superintendent Headley observed.

The question was raised, should they be treated so well? After all, this is not a school for girls. This is supposed to be prison.

"The best deterrent to crime is rehabilitation— self-rehabilitation with guidance," said one of the women in Fiske. "Someone is in prison because she didn't supervise her life properly in the past. If the guards and prison officials continue to supervise every action that an inmate takes, how is she really going to take charge of her life when she comes out? That's really in a way what Fiske is about."

At Fiske, they serve the same amount of time that they would if they were a part of the general prison population; they are still away from society, they still don't raise their children, they can't leave at night, but they can reflect on their life, they can acquire a skill, they can learn to live with other people peacefully, they can share and care. They can work toward a goal, and it costs a lot less money for the taxpayers.

Who are these people? They are all different. Several of them claim that they did not commit the crime for which they are serving time. In fact, that is different from male inmates who, more often, acknowledge their guilt. A lot of the Fiske women killed someone or were sentenced for an act that involved murder or manslaughter. While murder is the ultimate crime of violence, it is also the crime least likely to be repeated, particularly for women. Often, the woman who is accused of committing murder killed someone whom she knew, someone whom she was involved with, like an ex-lover, her husband, or her children. These are crimes that are not random, meaning that the woman did not go out on the street and deliberately kill a stranger or rob someone and unintentionally kill the victim. The women at Fiske are not considered career criminals—that is, the small number of people who commit a high percentage of violent crimes. So, what are prisons for—to rehabilitate or to punish? Fiske Cottage is not the answer for all prisoners, nor is it the answer for most prisoners, but perhaps this approach is the answer for some women and maybe some men.

Could this work for men? I asked the superintendent, who has worked within the prison system for many years.

He said no, he didn't think so.

But the idea of rehabilitation or change is only possible in an environment where the prisoners can feel a little bit like human beings.

"If I am not treated like a human being, then why should I ever change?" was the answer that one inmate gave me.

At Fiske, the trust level is so high that one of the women, who is the editor of the prison newspaper, has in her room a typewriter worth over a thousand dollars. It belongs to the institution, it is in her room, and no one thinks anything of it. I must say, I was surprised, but then again, these women would not destroy it because they feel that Fiske is their home.

She doesn't even lock the door, even though at Fiske the women have their own keys and can go in and out of their rooms as they please.

Everyone agrees that we should punish criminals. But how? Put them in prison? For how long? In what kind of prison? Which criminals? There are no easy answers, and there are no quick solutions. Fiske is an experiment for twenty-six women out of a prison population of almost a half million, of which less than 7 percent are women. The Fiske concept is just one alternative within one prison. It is a very different feeling being there, but it is still prison.

6

"WHITE-COLLAR" CRIME AND "STATE-RAISED" CONVICTS

"If I didn't have a family, I would really not mind. I really can't say that being in prison has been all that hard for me."

These are the words of Mike Shapiro, formerly an accountant in New York City, a man in his thirties, with a wife and a young child, serving a one-year sentence in a minimum-security facility.

Mike never in his life thought that he would be in prison. In fact, when they tried to build a prison near his elegant home, he fought it with the rest of his neighbors. He did not want criminals in his neighborhood. He never even knew people who had ever been in prison. If Mike was not in prison, he would be so ordinary that I would not be writing about him.

"I never heard of anyone being sent to prison for a 'white-collar' crime, except those famous politicians. White-collar crime used to be handled by good lawyers, who made deals with the prosecutor, and, after a

"White-collar" criminal Lew Bracker is shown getting
into his Mercedes at the Los Angeles County Jail
parking lot, on his way to work as a stockbroker.
At the end of the working day, he will return to jail.

cash settlement was made to the complainant, the whole matter was forgotten."

Mike is one of a group of people who committed a white-collar crime, got caught, and went to prison.* It seems that more and more people who commit that type of crime find themselves in prison, usually serving a short sentence. Most of them serve their time at minimum-security prisons in the country, some of which look like country clubs. Mike is in New York City, at a place that overlooks Central Park. It is not a country club, but it is not Greenhaven either. The security is certainly light. They don't have cells and brick walls, and they can have visitors daily. They can look out the window and see people walk their dogs, bicycle through the park, and see red and green traffic lights.

Mike is a very pleasant-looking guy; you can easily imagine him in a three-piece suit with a tie, a nice house, and a family. He looks like a man who could sit in an office all day, looking over figures. Well, that's what he did for years. He was a controller for a company that apparently had a very loose way of dealing with money. He was convicted of embezzling $250,000. He claims that he never took that much money, but since he used to sign the checks and authorize whatever expenses his bosses wanted, he got caught signing for things that apparently were not legitimate business expenses. Quietly, some people were stealing from the company with Mike's blessing. Since he was the controller, he was held responsible.

---

*"White-collar" crime was coined by Edwin Sutherland in a 1949 study of that section of the criminal population who were usually from the middle class and educated. The crimes are nonviolent and committed to acquire money, property, or other material goods. Usually these are crimes against companies rather than an individual, and often take years to detect.

He also helped himself to some of the profits, though he insists that it was not anywhere near $250,000.

"How could you get yourself into such a situation?" I wondered.

Mike shook his head. He said that he had been with the company for a long time, that everyone knew that some people were taking a little money on the side, and that he really didn't think that anyone would ever notice. Well, the auditors that came from the government did notice that the accounts did not balance. There seemed to be a great deal of money missing and, as Mike put it, he got caught because his signature was on the checks.

Mike has a devoted wife who comes to see him at least twice a week. His young child thinks that he is in a hospital, and his neighbors think that he accepted a good job out of town and will send for his family as soon as he gets settled. He spent the first part of his sentence working in the prison as a teacher. He kept himself busy with several jobs, reading, and teaching. In fact, he was afraid that if he continued teaching, they might fire the paid teacher and save money by having him teach high-school equivalency. Actually, he liked it. Now he works for the prison counselor, doing a lot of the clerical work that is part of operating a prison. Each inmate has a file that is as thick as a large-city phone book. He prepares the files for inmates concerning their daily pay (thirty-five cents or seventy-five cents a day, depending on the job). He keeps the record straight regarding their release date or their furlough date (a weekend pass), or to court. He works closely with the superintendent's office. He is almost like a staff member; his pay, though, is seventy-five cents a day.

Prison does not get him down too much. Since he will be ready for work release after serving six months of his sentence, Mike is sending out résumés for a job.

He does not give the prison as his return address, and he does not plan to inform his next boss where he has been the last year of his life. He will be moved shortly to a facility that has a work-release program, whereby inmates go out every day to work and come back at night to a "prison" or what is really a community-based house. They come back at night and go home on the weekends. Mike is now trying to work out how he will keep all his suits in his room when he starts working again. If all goes well, he will be paroled after he finishes his minimum sentence of one year, and once his parole is completed, he wants to leave the city and go somewhere else to start a new life. Of course, prison has taken a toll on him, and he says that although his wife has stood by him solidly, she is under a doctor's care because of the shock of the whole experience.

Middle-class prisoners like Mike are very much in the minority in prison. Prisons don't have a lot of college graduates; only 4 percent of the prison population completed college. Mike says that once this ordeal is all over, he would like to be a volunteer in prison and help prisoners with their education. He never wants to be a controller of a company again, and he does recognize that what he did was wrong.

"What did prison teach you?" I asked.

"I'll never do it again. The thing it taught me is that prisons are very badly run. I really can't believe sometimes how little is done for the inmates. There are very few programs, and the counselors hardly care about the inmates. Other than the work I do in prison, I keep very much to myself. I have very little to say to most of the people in here. We have nothing in common. So I just keep it that way."

The other extreme is a man named Jack Henry Abbott—a man who is considered to be a "state-raised" convict." Abbott became a famous prisoner after he wrote to a well-known writer, Norman Mailer. After exchanging letters with Mailer, he started writing about his experiences in prison. His book got a lot of attention. What he describes in his book as life in prison is nothing like Mike's life in prison.

Abbott was raised inside an institution. Since age twelve he has been free a total of only nine months. In his book, Abbott wrote about the kind of man one becomes after spending ten or twenty years in a maximum-security prison, much of it in solitary confinement, in the "hole." Abbott's story is horrifying. As a youth, he was in and out of foster homes. Because he could not adjust, he was sent to a juvenile institution. At age eighteen, he was convicted of writing a *bad check*. That's a check that you write when you don't have money in the bank to cover it. For that, he was sentenced to five years. While serving that sentence, he killed another inmate and was convicted of that crime. He is what's known as a "hard-core criminal," a man who would not know what it is really like to live in the outside world, or what the customs are of a society.

Abbott is exceptional in that he educated himself while in prison, though that may not be so exceptional, since he spent so much time in solitary confinement where there is not much for an inmate to do but read and write. Perhaps what is more remarkable is that he wrote about his experiences. In Abbott's descriptions of the prisons he was in, violence was a way of life. People who have been caged in for years lose all humanity, and live by a prison code that is the most horrifying, the fear of being killed by either an inmate or by a guard at any time. Abbott describes prison as the most terrible place, a place that seems like an insane asylum, a place where the inmates are treated with brutality by the guards, where the guards permit and encourage rapes, where drugs are bought and sold, sometimes with sexual favors, where the inmates have no regard for each other or for human life, where survival is only possible once an inmate establishes that he will kill, if necessary.

Abbott wrote the following:

> After ten years, the sun never sets nor rises in a prison. There are no seasons; no wind or rain or sunlight in your hair. There are no children to give you a vision of life, no women to comfort your soul. I have never walked beneath the sky at nighttime on prison grounds . . . You can't stand the sight of each other and yet you are doomed to stand and face one another every moment of every day for years without end. You must bathe together, defecate and urinate together, eat and sleep together, talk together, work together.

Abbott was paroled after his book was published, with a lot of support from numerous famous people who felt that, through his book, he had made a major literary contribution to society. Within months of his release from prison, he stabbed a person to death. The man who had spent most of his life in prison is back in prison again.

There are others like Abbott who have been in prison for a very long time; many of them have killed. But if Abbott's description is to be believed, life in prison is like life in a jungle, with nothing like love, care, or concern, or even a glimpse of what our life is like on the outside. What are we releasing from prison? Are they human beings? Can they cross the street with the light? Do they know how to turn on a stove? Can they cook a meal? Would they know how to get on a subway or drive a car? Can they resolve a conflict without resorting to violence?

So, that's who is in prison. There are people like Mike Shapiro and then some are like Jack Abbott. Some have been put in prison for passing a bad check and have, while there, become killers; and others, like Mike, are accused of taking a lot of money from a company. Mike Shapiro and Jack Abbott have had different experiences in prison. They served time in very different places, and they were very different people before they entered prison. And if prisons are the way that Abbott describes them, then we really have to worry about those people coming out. They are a serious threat to society. How can they be expected to function outside of prison? They really never have.

As Abbott put it, "To be in prison so long it's difficult to remember exactly what you did to get there." You think of your future, a future you know can never exist.

7

THE FIRST OFFENDER

I was sitting with a group of men at Lincoln Correctional Facility in New York City, a minimum-security prison, talking about "the kids" coming to prison.

"What should we do about sixteen-year-olds who have committed serious crimes?" I asked.

"Put them in prison," was the response of Steve, a man who spent eighteen years in and out of prison, since he was about seventeen years old. "The problem is that if you don't take these crimes seriously, these kids continue to think that it's a joke. I say, let them see what it's like to be locked up every night in a cell by yourself."

The men in this group were very divided about how they felt about "kids" in prison. John, who is serving time for armed robbery, and has been in prison for many years, vehemently disagreed.

"How can you say that, when you know what happens to these kids? First they are raped by somebody, then they learn to be tough guys, learn to commit all sorts of crimes, listen to the stories that these guys tell them, and they go out there really angry and act like animals. No! There is really hope for these kids. They should never be thrown in prison. They should be put into a special program, they should be sent to a half-way house, they should get an education. Prison will do nothing but make them into better criminals."

The problem of "kids" going to prison is an ever-growing concern. First, the number of juveniles, or people under eighteen years old, committing crimes, is on the rise. The age of the so-called first offender is getting lower and lower and crimes that they commit are more and more serious. The controversy about what to do with them is growing: some people believe that the best deterrent to juvenile crime is prison; others believe that juvenile offenders can be rehabilitated, and should be helped.

Henry is eighteen years old now, having served almost two years in prison for robbery and assault. He has been out of prison and out of "trouble" for eighteen months. He is shy and soft-spoken, and has warm brown eyes.

"You robbed somebody?" I asked.

"Well, actually, I didn't, but I was there."

Henry then told me a little about how he got involved with the street life. Henry grew up in the Bronx, in New York City, in an area where almost every building has been burned out. Some buildings have no heat, some have no windows. Most of them are rat-infested, with ceilings falling down. The women are on welfare, the children play in the streets, and drugs are sold openly. Henry's parents were divorced, though he maintained a strong relationship with his father, who remarried and had several other children.

"My mother tried to talk to me, always told me

that I would get into trouble, but I really didn't listen to her. My mother had no control over me by the time I was twelve years old. I stopped going to school about that time and just started hanging out on the streets. I began drinking and using drugs—'reefers.' When we committed this robbery, I was high on marijuana and alcohol."

Henry seemed unsure as to what really happened. He said that he and his friends decided to rob someone. They robbed a man on the street and assaulted him. The police arrived before the incident was over.

"You can imagine how sophisticated we were. We rob this guy in front of the cops."

Henry was arrested and sent to a prison in upstate New York.

"It's not that I liked prison, but it was good for me. I was scared but I kept to myself. Prison does things to you. It made me face my life and where I was headed. I also saw what it did to my family. It really hurt my father to the point that it was hard for him to see me. I talked a lot to the older guys and some of them tried to help me. But I tell you one thing for sure. Prison is an education in crime. You learn to commit crimes in a way that you never did before. I knew that crime was not for me. I still love the streets, though. I like the excitement, the energy."

Henry was released from prison with the stipulation that he receive job training. He enrolled in Project Real, a small, unique eight-week program, in which youngsters learn how to use a computer, prepare for their high school equivalency test, and get job training and counseling. Henry is one of the success stories. He learned how to use a computer and, like most youngsters, he loved it. He is preparing to take his high school equivalency test and now has a job as a shipping clerk.

But Henry is still not out of the woods. A lot of

pressure is on him. He is concerned about his father who is going to be operated on for lung cancer. But the thing that is also bothering him deeply is that his girl-friend is pregnant and will be giving birth within the next two months, something that Henry is clearly unprepared for.

"I guess that we'll try to find an apartment and I'll have to get a second job, and we'll try to make it some-how. I am scared. Right now she's living with her mother, and I try to see her in the evenings. I am try-ing to save enough money for the baby."

While Henry was talking, I caught a faraway look in his eyes.

"How could you get yourself into this situation before you could get yourself on an even keel?" I asked.

Henry just shook his head. He was very much aware that his problems were overwhelming. At times he feels ready to give up. "Ready to give up," he kept repeating—a "kid" out of prison less than two years and now about to become a father.

"I really am scared. I just have too much stuff to work out. I really don't know how this is going to work for us," he said with a sigh.

"Have you thought about having your girlfriend stay with her mother for a while longer? Maybe it would work better that way."

Henry liked that idea, and, several hours later, he had decided he would present the idea to his girl-friend, knowing that she would not like it.

"She is really looking forward to our living together. She'll be disappointed."

Henry was clearly very committed to his girl-friend, but he was not nearly ready for a family. Obviously, Henry still could not deal with all the pres-sures of being out of prison.

"You know, I had to learn how to cross the streets

all over again. I feel that if too much is put on me, I'll just withdraw. Sometimes I just sit on the rooftop and think. I really would like to do so many things. I would like to go back to school, I love my girlfriend, I want to marry her one day, I really don't want to leave her with a kid. I feel so frightened sometimes."

As I left Henry, I strongly urged him to get counseling. He needed help. He accepted my advice and went to talk to his counselor at Project Real. The hard road is still ahead for Henry, but I think that he'll make it. What fascinated me is that I could not imagine this youngster with a gun, or hurting anyone, but I could see how he could get pulled into situations. He is vulnerable and scared—a perfect victim for someone to lead almost anywhere. In the past, he followed the wrong crowd. He is still capable of that.

Winston was the same age as Henry. He never went to prison, although he pleaded guilty to a charge of assault. Winston beat up his girlfriend's father with a baseball bat, an injury that required over twenty stitches.

"Why?"

"Well, I beat him because he threatened me. He told me that if ever I came to see his daughter, he would kill me. Meanwhile he abused his daughter and hurt her, so I decided that I should retaliate. So he pressed charges. I pleaded guilty and got a two-year probation with the stipulation that I go into a program."

Winston had no previous record of arrest, and had never been in trouble with the law, so the judge felt that he didn't need to be punished by serving time in prison. There was no indication that he was dangerous to society. He had a quick temper and seemed to feel that it was his duty to play the manly role of his girlfriend's protector.

"Are you sorry about what you did?" I asked.

"No! He had hurt the woman I love. Also, he threatened me first."

"What if you had to go to prison?"

"Well, that might have been different. I know that I have a bad temper and I have to deal with that. I can't go beating people up, but he really abused her."

Winston has completed the same program in which Henry was enrolled. Winston passed his high school equivalency exam, is scheduled to go to college in the fall, and has a job at an elegant clothing store in New York City. Winston is an example of someone who benefited by enrolling in a small program where people cared about him and where counselors talked to him about his violent temper. Within less than two years, he is on his way to getting off probation. He is still with the same girlfriend. He worries about saving money, moving out of his aunt's house, going to school full time, and being able to keep his job. The prison experience would have been frightening to him and in no way would it have dealt with his problem of controlling his temper. If anything, he would have learned that violent behavior is the normal way of life in prison.

Patsy was not so fortunate. She is serving time at Bedford Hills Correctional Facility. Now twenty years old, she has been there for three years. Patsy was not from the city, unlike so many of the other juveniles. Coming from a middle-class background, she was pampered by her family. She dropped out of school at an early age. Patsy is cute and charming, with a shy smile. She spent her time with a group of youngsters who were involved in drugs, robbing people, and living the so-called "street life." They committed senseless crimes, stealing money, snatching gold chains, and acting "mean" and "tough." That's very important on the streets.

"You have to be tough—that's how you get people to look up to you," according to Patsy.

She became increasingly involved with drugs, staying out at night, and "running the streets," as she called it. One night she was out with a group of friends, and ran into a girl who bothered her.

"What do you mean by 'bothered you'?" I asked.

"She kept looking at me, staring at me. So we got into an argument. I took out my knife from my bag and stabbed her once and then I left. I really didn't think that anything serious had happened. Later that night, I was watching television and this bulletin came on the news that a fifteen-year-old girl was stabbed to death. I almost fainted. I had no idea that I had done that! I never planned to kill her. So I told my grandmother what had happened. I walked into the police station and turned myself in. I got three to seven years."

At seventeen, Patsy went to prison pregnant. She gave birth in prison, and kept her baby with her for a year, the maximum time allowed.

"That really changed me—taking care of her in here. She's with my grandmother now. But I see her a few times a month. My family comes to see me, and they bring the baby. Can you imagine giving birth in a hospital, and when you leave, they handcuff you and bring you back to prison? You can't even hold your own baby. The guard brings your baby." (Bedford Hills is one of the few prisons that has a facility for babies, up to one year.)

"How do you feel about spending your teenage years in prison?"

"No one likes being in prison, but it's probably the best thing that happened to me. I think that I would have died out there on those streets. I was moving fast and getting into more and more trouble. So this experience helped me get myself together. When you think about giving birth in prison, and when you see your kid being taken away, I guess some reality sets in."

Patsy was treated well by the other women. The women tend to treat the younger inmates much better than the men do. They tend to assume a mothering role for the younger women.

Patsy will be released from prison soon. She is a bit scared and very unsure about what she will do.

"I want to take care of my baby. If I do that for the next year, that's about all that I want. Also, I want to get out of town. I came from a small town, and I don't want this stigma to live with me forever. Every night I used to wake up in a sweat from a nightmare. I know that I will forever have to live with the fact that I killed someone. All I want is a quiet life and maybe to get married someday."

I asked Patsy what advice she had for kids her age.

"It's so easy to get into trouble—to get into a crowd with kids who smoke pot, drink, and just do things because they think that it's cool. It's being a Mr. Big Guy. It's macho! Then in a second all that fun turns into a nightmare. It's not worth it. It's better to be 'square' than to end up spending your life trying to piece it back together."

Patsy weighed about ninety pounds and in no way looked like she could be a threat to anyone. But an incident that took only a moment, took the life of a fifteen-year-old girl, and Patsy will live with that pain for the rest of her life.

"If you had not been high, do you think that you would have stabbed her?"

"No. I can't remember what really happened. My mind was in a haze. I was not thinking or even realized that the knife in my pocket could kill."

And that's how a lot of innocent people die.

Not everyone who comes out of prison feels like Patsy. Not all of the youngsters come out feeling that prison gave them a place to stay off drugs, off the streets, and a place to think. The term "first offender" is misleading, because most of the prisoners under eighteen years of age have usually committed numerous crimes before serving their first sentence in prison. When they go to prison, they think that they are very rough and tough. But much of the youth crime is considered by the older prisoners to be "punklike"—beating up somebody for ten dollars or taking someone's necklace, smoking marijuana, drinking all night, or defying their parents. When these youngsters enter jail, very often the older prisoners like to impress them with stories that they can't even imagine taking place. Some of the men, particularly those who have become hardened, who like to brag, love to tell the younger population some of these horror stories (some of which are highly imaginary). For many of the youngsters, this is the first real exposure to criminals and criminal activities that are more than petty thefts to buy a new pair of sneakers or go to the movies. Some of them learn about robbing banks in a professional manner, how to be "real" pimps, how to be runners for a drug dealer, or sell their own bodies.

Running drugs for a drug dealer is very common. Because the drug laws in most states are far more lenient toward people under eighteen than for adults, young people are used to sell the drugs or deliver them from one part of the city to another.

Joe's story is not untypical. He left school at age sixteen before getting a high-school diploma. He looked very mature for his age, but his reading level was about fourth grade. His mother had no control over him; his father had abandoned the family when

Joe was a child, so long ago that he can't remember. His older brother tried to talk some sense into him, but all Joe saw on the streets was fast money—fast money from drugs, from women, and from other illegal activities. He rarely went home at night; if he did, his mother was already asleep.

When I talked to his mother about Joe, she was not emotional about Joe being in prison. In a way, she felt that prison was good for him.

"I tried to talk to him, I tried everything, but there is no way to talk to that kid. Maybe once he sees what it's like to be locked up every night and be told what to do every minute of the day, he'll come to his senses."

Joe thought that he was a tough guy when he first went to prison. He felt that he didn't need anybody.

"Man, they told me that I needed protection, that I needed to get into a group, but I knew that I was tough. After all, I am in here for beating a man to near death," he bragged to me.

In a matter of weeks, he was raped by a gang of men, and two weeks later, after he reported the incident to the guards, he was stabbed in the prison yard. He was not seriously hurt, needing only a few stitches, but he got into fights with other inmates who decided to retaliate because he informed on them. He also got into fights with the guards because he didn't like the way they talked to him.

One of the older inmates chuckled, "He was a hard nut to crack. He really thought that he was a big shot, so some of the guys in here showed him how tough he really was. He didn't understand how to deal with the guards. Well, you have to learn how to get along with them. If you show them no respect, they can give it back to you in a thousand ways. I mean, you might be dying, but they will take their time about taking you to the nurse. Poor Joe, he learned the hard way. He didn't understand that some of the guys in here are real criminals. They ain't playing."

Joe was placed in isolation for a month. He was allowed out of his cell for one hour a day for exercise—when the other inmates weren't around. He was in a little cell for twenty-three hours a day, all alone.

Joe can't sleep at night, he hears voices. He wakes up screaming sometimes, and he is afraid to come out of prison. He sees a psychiatrist who helps him, but Joe's experiences have left deep emotional scars. He was not the tough guy that he thought he was, and just being locked up made him claustrophobic (morbidly fearful of being in a confined space). He fears that there will be a fire one night and the guards will run out and leave all the prisoners locked in.

Joe joined the Black Muslims, a group that is orderly and concerned about living a religious and legal life outside of prison. They are among the best prisoners—courteous, well-behaved, and disciplined. They tend to be very highly respected by other inmates and exercise a lot of control over the other inmates while also practicing some very strong discipline concerning dietary laws. After Joe joined them, he was left alone by the other inmates, but now he had to listen to the Black Muslim leadership. He had to go to school, read the Koran (which is like the Bible), and not eat pork, among other restrictions.

"After I joined with them guys, I never went anywhere alone. I stuck with those guys. I was scared. I really thought that I would be killed in here. Sometimes I would cry because I didn't want to die. I swear, I felt like this was a place of death."

"Why didn't you join them earlier?" I asked.

"Are you kidding? I didn't want to have all those rules and regulations, I had no idea about that religion. I didn't even go to church. I am not sure that I really believe in a God. I joined because I was scared and they made some sense to me; they were different from the other guys. They seemed like they were trying to make something of their lives. They have saved my life."

"So, what are you most afraid of now?"

"Getting out," was the answer.

Joe is still in prison. He is still trying to cope with the psychological effects of the rape.

"You know that for a while I didn't know if I was a man or a woman. That's how deeply those guys affected me. I am just coming out of all that. For a while I didn't even know if I wanted to live. I thought about suicide a lot. Now I am taking it one day at a time."

"What would you tell kids about being in prison or getting into trouble?" I wanted to know.

"You can't tell them anything. You couldn't tell me anything. They have to experience this for themselves. It's survival."

"Kids" in prison! The very idea seems like a contradiction in terms.

8

DEATH ROW

There are over eleven hundred people on "death row" in America. Some have been living that way for years, some only for a few months. They may never be executed or they may die tomorrow.

The people on death row are usually convicted of first-degree murder. They are accused of committing some frightening, some unbelievably gruesome crimes. Some admit to these killings, and yet some of the others claim to be innocent. The death-row prisoners live in isolation, in total segregation from the rest of the prison population. They are in cells that are separated and removed from the rest of the facility. The cells are close to the execution room—usually just down the hall. The cells are about six-by-nine feet; they are empty of any furniture, other than a cot, a sink, and a toilet. A death-row inmate may have a color television in the cell, or a television is affixed to the wall outside the cell so that it can be seen through the cell window. Through the window the inmate can also see the corridor. The guard, who is stationed there twenty-four hours a day, lights the inmate's cigarettes, and brings the meals and mail. In some prisons the inmate is taken out of the cell for about an hour a day and into the prison yard where all that can be seen is the sky and high stone walls. That is all. That is life on death row day in and day out. The inmate is not allowed to see anyone but family, his or her lawyer, and the clergy. Death-row inmates cannot eat or talk with anyone at all. They have no work assignments around the prison; they can't go to school. Death row is set up for one purpose—to hold a person until execution. The prison is required only to house, feed, and then kill the inmate.

Nineteen sixty-seven was the year of the last execution before a ten-year hiatus, when in 1977 Gary Gilmore died amidst a good deal of controversy and outrage. The number of people awaiting execution is the highest ever recorded since 1953 when the national count was first taken. The legal issues concerning capital punishment are very complex, and often diffi-

One hand, signaling "thumbs up," was extended through the bars of a death row cell in Angola State Penitentiary in Louisiana, when forty men awaiting execution were reprieved by a United States Supreme Court ruling that the death penalty was "cruel and unusual" punishment and unconstitutional.

cult for the lay person to grasp. But some of the issues are very interesting and penetrating. In 1972, the United States Supreme Court ruled in an historic case, *Furman v. Georgia*, that the death penalty had often been used in an arbitrary and capricious manner, thereby violating the Eighth and Fourteenth Amendments that prohibit cruel and unusual punishment. All of the six hundred persons sentenced under the pre-Furman law and awaiting death were eventually removed from death row. That should give you a sense of how very fragile life on death row really is. Imagine, that you are in a cell awaiting execution, and the United States Supreme Court decides that the manner in which capital punishment has been practiced violates the Constitution, that in fact, because of a legal loophole, you are *not* going to die. However, the Supreme Court did not say that capital punishment was in itself unconstitutional. There is a difference. What the Court said was that capital punishment was constitutional but that the way in which it was carried out was not. The justices said that there had to be very strict laws governing this issue and that the state laws had to be consistent. In a sense, the Furman case opened the door for new state laws while it struck down the existing ones. Although this decision was a major defeat for those hoping that the court would declare capital punishment itself to be unconstitutional, it did slow down the execution process. The new state laws now had to incorporate several elements to make certain that procedures for carrying out capital punishment would no longer be arbitrary.

For example, a person in Mississippi, let's say, cannot be sentenced to die in an electric chair for a robbery, while a person in Minnesota is given a life sentence for murdering ten people. Now, the Court approved the following procedures: there must first be a trial on the issue of guilt or innocence; if the defendent is found guilty of murder, a separate trial must be conducted on the issue of life or death. In other words, the person may be guilty, but whether or not he or she is to be sentenced to death is a separate issue. Also, with the new Court decision, all capital punishment cases require a jury trial. Ordinarily, many cases are resolved by guilty pleas and the state is spared the expense of a trial. About 85 percent of the cases used to end in that manner. Now, a jury must decide the issue of guilt, before a person can be sentenced to death.

Most of the states have new laws that are consistent with the Supreme Court decision, and therefore a lot of people have been added to death row since 1976, awaiting appeals at one level or another. At this point some of the people on death row can take their pleas from one court to another for review, and their execution could be put off for a few years. They are entitled to an automatic appeal with a death sentence. Very recently, the Supreme Court has changed that process, by accelerating the process of appeals. All the same, a person on death row can wait for years to find out if the courts will grant a stay of execution. They live this way, in total isolation. The only thing that they can do is read a lot and write a lot. Usually the death-row inmates are extremely knowledgeable about their cases, and even those who may have less than a tenth-grade education can explain legal complexities in great detail and with sophistication.

I met Edward Durre at Colorado State Correctional Facility, at Canon City, Colorado. Durre is a big, white, heavyset man, who looks a little older than his age. In his mid-forties, he has a thirty-year history of crime. I didn't realize at the time we met that spending a few hours out of his cell was a special experience for him. He was waiting for me, anxious to talk. He talked almost nonstop for several hours. He brought with him his court records, far too long for anyone to read in one sitting. Durre wanted to tell me about his thirty years of crime. He admitted to being a crook, even a career criminal, but he did not admit to the crime for which he was sentenced—first-degree murder. His past record related to all types of criminal activities involving property and getting money, a lot of money, quickly. Durre was no angel. He didn't even seem to feel so terrible about his very long list of criminal activities. I was amazed that he could remember most of the crimes for which he was arrested, and where and when he served his time. Durre was not only articulate but also very knowledgeable about the legalities of his case and possible loopholes in the law.

Durre's childhood was unlike that of a lot of prisoners who come from economically deprived backgrounds. Durre admits to being spoiled by his grandmother at a very early age. He says he got whatever he wanted, and he wanted a lot of material things. So, as he got older and his grandmother was no longer willing to give him money, he resorted to crime as a fast way of getting what he wanted. I should mention that Durre was married and divorced five times in the midst of his life of crime and serving time in prison.

As he tells it, his oldest son, after many years of absence, returned to be with his father. His son, whom he had hardly known during the early years, was apparently involved in his own type of criminal activity. According to Durre, his son preyed on homosexuals, robbing them of money or whatever property he could get from them. In 1981, the body of a young man was found in the basement of Durre's house; he had been brutally stabbed numerous times. Durre claims that he was not involved in the crime, that he was not even aware that his son had brought someone there, but that when he came home, he found some bloody sheets that he then quickly disposed of.

Now, the rest of the story sounds like a poor, trashy novel. Later, when Durre and his son were arrested, his son implicated his father in the murder. Durre claims that his son was seeking revenge for Durre leaving his mother and deserting the family. Why did Durre dispose of the sheets instead of calling the police? Durre argues that a man with a criminal record like his would not usually call the police to report a crime. I, of course, do not know the answer to those questions. I do not know if Durre is guilty as charged. His son got a long sentence but, in consideration of his age and because he was not considered a career criminal, he was not given the death sentence.

Durre's case is being appealed; it may take years before he is actually executed. His spirit certainly reflected that feeling.*

"How do you feel about sitting here and not knowing if you are going to die?"

Durre's answer was one of confidence. He vehemently upholds his innocence and believes that he will get a new trial.

I talked to some of the prison staff who are responsible for inmates on death row. They said that Durre's confidence is common among inmates, anyhow during the earlier period on death row. First, in any case, with those inmates who claim their innocence, there is a good deal of optimism, and they spend their time educating themselves about their case so they know that they have several legal recourses and at least a

*In May 1984, the Colorado Supreme Court ruled that the judge who tried Durre's case gave flawed instructions to the jury, and that Durre's death sentence was to be nullified and replaced with a sentence of life in prison.

few years before the death penalty will be carried out. However, according to the staff, after years of isolation in a cell six-by-nine feet, some of the inmates have begun to show signs of insanity, and others have become very religious. Some have committed suicide.

Even on death row, the inmates are different from one another. The main thing they have in common is that they are accused of first-degree murder. While Durre is accused of one man's death, Lemuel Smith, the only inmate on death row in New York State, is at Greenhaven, the maximum-security prison, convicted of the murder and rape of a correctional officer while he was in prison for committing several other murders. However, in New York State, the law makes the death penalty a possibility when a person already serving a life sentence commits another murder.

Like Durre, Lemuel Smith claims to be innocent.

Smith was released at age thirty-six from Greenhaven in 1976—he had been in prison for more than half his life. In the ten months that followed, according to his criminal record, he killed four people, three of them women, and abducted and raped a fifth.

Lemuel Smith has been killing since he was sixteen years old. Clearly, he is a man dangerous to society. His legal case is complex, but one thing that everyone seemed to agree on is that Lemuel Smith was crazy when he committed the murders. He seemed unable to recall some of them. In fact, he seemed to have been anxious to receive psychiatric help, being aware that there was something seriously wrong with him. However, he was never placed in a hospital. He remained at Greenhaven.

Smith also does not remember the last killing—the murder of a female guard in the chapel of the prison. How he got there, how he managed to be alone with a female guard, how he managed to get rid of the body and dump it in the garbage are all questions that no one has been able to answer. Apparently though, Smith was likable and a good prisoner, so he had a lot of leeway in prison. Like many inmates, he was an artist; apparently he knew the guard and tried to sell her some of his work. That's what some people have said.

Lemuel Smith is an important case. He, unlike Durre, has a long history of murder and rape. He is also a man who is clearly "crazy." He cannot be out on the streets, but the question is whether he belongs in prison, whether he should be killed by the state, or whether he should be in a hospital for the criminally insane. Should society attempt to treat a man like this or is the death penalty the answer?

To keep people on death row is expensive. First, there is the cost of trials and appeals. Then, because an inmate on death row is kept in isolation and has his own guard twenty-four hours a day, the cost of the inmate's upkeep is high.

Someone once wrote a "want ad" for death row:

Applicant Wanted: DEATH ROW

Suitable applicants must be male, approximately 31 years of age, undereducated and economically deprived. Should have murdered a white person and be represented by court-appointed counsel. No prior experience necessary, drug and/or alcohol helpful. Must be willing to spend numerous years under psychological stress, live in a barren environment, and die in a prearranged manner.

Well, that description is not far from the truth. We have approximately eleven hundred people on death row, though that figure changes all the time. Twelve of those are females. Of the total, 52 percent are white and 42 percent are black, 4 percent Hispanic, and the rest are "other." Most of them murdered someone white, and a very large percentage did not have their own attorney, but had a lawyer who was appointed by the court.

In 1977, after ten years during which this country did not have any executions, Gary Gilmore was put to death by firing squad. Previously, while on death row, he attempted suicide twice. The thirty-six-year-old Gilmore was sentenced for the shooting death of a Utah motel clerk. Gilmore became well-known at the time—first, because he was the first to be executed in many years, and second, because he did not fight the execution. His last words were, "Let's do it." Gilmore's action raised the question of whether some people on death row welcome their own death rather than live in a six-by-nine foot cell for the rest of their lives. He also seemed to be suicidal.

Another man, Bishop, was executed in 1979, refusing to appeal his case, and accepting his death. The same year, however, in Florida, a man who fought his case to the end, John Spenkelink, lost, and was put to death in an electric chair.

Capital punishment is not unique to the United States. In Western Europe, only France and Spain still apply capital punishment in peacetime. Britain, after eight hundred years of hanging criminals, abolished the death penalty for most crimes in 1969. Almost all the Arab and African countries have the death penalty. The death penalty exists in South America, the Soviet Union, Eastern Europe, as well as everywhere in Asia.

Many people oppose the death penalty on moral and religious grounds. Some feel that it is murder, while others argue that the state should not have the license to kill. Still others argue that there is no point in keeping people alive in isolation in a tiny cell. Certainly, many people on death row will agree that life there is not very much of a life. However, one argument that some people raise is the Zimmerman case. Isadore Zimmerman was in prison for twenty-five years. He was scheduled to die. His sentence was later reversed; he received a new trial and was found innocent. Once released from prison, he sued the state and eighteen years later was awarded a million dollars for the injustice he had suffered.* Well, people will argue, what about people like him? Maybe some of the other people on death row who claim that they are innocent really are. Should we take that chance and possibly kill an innocent man?

The writer Doug Magee described the execution of John Spenkelink, who died in 1979 in Florida.

Just after ten o'clock on the morning of Friday, May 25, 1979, John Spenkelink was wrestled from his cell in the Q wing of the Florida State Prison by six guards and carried struggling to a small room down the hall. His head and right calf had been shaved forcibly, and he was gagged because he had shouted, "This is murder, this is murder!" In the center of the small room where he was taken was a three-legged oak instrument: the electric chair.

Wearing a white shirt with rolled-up sleeves, Spenkelink was strapped into the chair at the arms, legs, and chest. His mouth and chin were covered by a black muzzle

*Zimmerman died in 1983. Of the one million dollars he received, he had spent less than a thousand of it.

wrapped around his neck. A white towel, wrapped round his throat, secured his head to the back of the chair. The guards put a wet sponge on his head to conduct electricity better and then fitted a metal cap over the sponge. A black hood was drawn half over his head while the two black electrical cords that snaked out of a box on the wall behind the chair were connected to his body.

Before him he could see a plate glass window covered by a curtain running the length of the wall. To his right was an anteroom with a slit of window cut in the anteroom wall. Through the slit he could see two hooded men; one would be his executioner. The guards stood around the chair. The tight muzzle bulged his cheeks, but he could see the movement of the curtain on the large window in front of him as it opened. He caught a brief glimpse of the witnesses behind the glass, as they did of him, before the hood was dropped quickly over his face.

Within seconds, what must have been horrible seconds for him, massive amounts of electricity jolted his body. Three doses in all. Smoke curled up from the burning flesh on the

The night before the execution of condemned killer John Spenkelink, the sun sets behind Q wing (death row) of the Florida State Prison at Raiford.

inside of his thigh and his fingers, gripping the flat armrest, curled backward in convulsion. He was dead.

I did not watch John Spenkelink's execution. I stood with the rest of the press in a fenced-in meadow across from the flat, green buildings of the Florida State Prison and listened first to the radio reports and then to the accounts of the witnesses and pool reporters. In the glare of bright midmorning sun I had trouble realizing that not more than three hundred yards from where I stood a man I had come to know well in the eight months since I had first photographed him for a magazine article had been taken into an execution chamber and killed.

As I listened to the details of his death, his last statement played in my head like a broken record. His lawyers had to bring the statement out to the press; the prison authorities would not allow him to speak for himself. He said he wanted the governor to come and meet him, to sit and talk with him like a human being. Many who heard those words thought they were preposterous. To me they sounded like common sense.

A cream-colored hearse carried John Spenkelink's body away from the prison. The big car sped into town—and I looked past the line of state troopers, the big open field, the barbed wire, and double chain link fence to the prison. Those green buildings, swimming in the warm air of a late spring morning, stayed with me for days. The distance between us and the 133 other men left on death row now seemed immense, unbridgeable.

I came to see the accuracy of that image. I realized, after looking into capital punishment more deeply, that the information we get about people on death row most often comes from intermediaries: lawyers, court records, journalists, and social scientists. Like the people on death rows throughout the country, the people in the R and Q wings of the Florida State Prison are cut off from us and we from them.

Prison authorities say there are security reasons for this distance. I think it goes deeper than that. If the people on death row are allowed to speak for themselves, if they become human before us, we have to face the hard fact that we are executing human beings.*

*Reprinted with permission. Copyright 1980, Christianity and Crisis, 537 West 121 Street, New York, New York 10027.

9

ALTERNATIVES

Are there alternatives to prison? The fact is that most offenders are not in prison: 4 percent of persons under correctional supervision are in the community on probation or parole. Probation provides conditional liberty in the community. Essentially, while on probation, a person can receive a jail sentence for even the most minor violation of the law. The probation officer assigned to the case checks to see that the person does not violate the conditions of his or her probation. Probation is by far the most prevalent prison alternative. Currently, 1.2 million people are on probation. *Parole* means community supervision after release from prison or jail. It is intended to ease the transition to the outside life.

Other than probation or parole, halfway houses are the most common forms of alternatives that we have to prison. I guess that just like the words *death row, halfway house* is also a very appropriate name for what it is. It is a place halfway between prison and the so-called outside world. There are no cells, no security guards, no metal detectors to walk through, no searches, no locked doors, but there is a curfew, there is a staff to provide counseling, and there are rules to be followed.

Greenhope, located in an old convent in one of the worst areas in New York City, is most probably one of the best examples of a good halfway house for women. The women who are sent to Greenhope have served their time in prison, usually in a maximum-security facility. They come to Greenhope either at the end of their sentence or when they are paroled. There are usually about twenty residents, a real change from an institution that had five hundred or six hundred inmates. Greenhope has single rooms for the women and a large dining area where they eat together. Some halfway houses have a hired cook, but in others, the residents take turns cooking and cleaning up in the kitchen. While at Greenhope, the women go to school during the day or they have a job. At night they come back for counseling and to sleep. On the weekends they can stay out till two or three in the morning or even overnight if they have prior approval from the staff.

These halfway houses are not meant to house people for a very long period of time: six months to a year. When I met Sandra at one of these places, she had already served three years in a maximum-security prison for drug possession. She came out feeling very lost but determined to rebuild her life.

According to a halfway house counselor, "One of the biggest problems . . . is that they want to do everything at once. So, many of them come out and the very first weekend they come back drunk and then they have to be put on probation. Then they want to have a job by the second week and they don't want to realize that it takes time."

Sandra, as well as several other inmates just released, confirmed this statement. Yes, they have been locked up for years and now that they have so much freedom, it's difficult to handle. Therefore, the first task of the staff is to help the residents realize that everything will not happen immediately. Before the counselors send anyone out for a job or even to be trained, they encourage a lot of talking and planning a course of action that will be the best for the resident in the long run. They recognize that the road back is long and it needs to be carefully planned. The favorite saying is that if you have a lifetime for committing crimes and years to spend in prison, you should have at least a few months to get yourself together.

Sandra's was a success story. She did take her situation one day at a time. She first decided that she needed some vocational training and enrolled in a school that taught data processing. She finished her training and got a job. Although she earns very little money, she is learning how to budget it, something that she had never done before. She now has a bank account and can balance a checkbook, a major change in her life. Her second task was to begin to mend the relationship that she had with her children. She sees them regularly, has learned to play with them, and take them to interesting places. Now that she has been at a halfway house for eight months, she is making preparations to look for a place to stay and to buy furniture with the money she saves.

"It takes time," Sandra said. "They kept telling me that it would take a lot of time, and it does. That's one thing that is so hard to believe and understand, but to get yourself together does take time and if you rush it or if you get overly anxious, then you just get all crazy and you blow the whole thing. It really is a delicate balancing act. Just to get over prison takes a year. I still have nightmares. I still hear the clinking of keys, the locking and unlocking of cells, the noise. I am just beginning to sleep."

Then, of course, there is always retribution as an alternative to prison. I talked to a judge who said, "I never could see what prison will do for some type of offender. Maybe they need to spend some time in prison, but basically, I think that if a kid burglarized an apartment, or broke into a car, he should have to pay back what he has taken. I believe that, particularly with juvenile offenders, if there is property involved, they should have to pay for the damage."

For property crimes, retribution provides a way for the offender to compensate the victim for what has been taken or destroyed. The retribution concept has been taken to another level in some of the Scandinavian countries, where an offender not only has to replace the property that has been taken or destroyed, but in some cases, must work for the victim in some capacity to repay the debt. One of the problems of retribution in this country is that most of the people in prison do not have the necessary skills, first to get a job and then earn the money to repay the victim. The problem is compounded in the case of heroin addicts who steal several times a day to support their habit.

Some people have suggested that heroin addicts should not go to prison but should be treated for their illness, since drug addiction is an illness. Again, the problem with that notion is that there are hundreds of thousands of drug addicts in this country, and many of them have already been in treatment programs that did not seem to work for them very well. So what do we do with them?

Parole provides for the release of a prisoner after the minimum sentence has been served and with the approval of the parole board. However, there are a lot of problems with the idea of parole. When appearing before the parole committee the prisoner must present a plan explaining what he or she intends to do upon release from prison. In the granting of parole, an inmate's prison behavior is taken into account, but there is no way that the parole committee can be sure that even the best prisoners will make it on the outside. First, some of the best prisoners are very adaptable to the prison structure; when they are released, they cannot function well at all. Second, even the best of plans, once tested on the outside, can fall apart. Inmates who come out of prison are emotionally vulnerable, and can find their way back into old lifestyles at the slightest difficulty. After all, if they had managed their lives better, they would not be in trouble with the law and not have gone to prison.

Probation is another alternative to prison. As mentioned earlier, well over a million people are on probation. This alternative enables people who have been convicted of minor offenses to live in society as long as they are on good behavior.*

Some judges sentence offenders to weekend trips to prison. That means that an offender is able to hold a job, but is still punished by spending weekends locked inside a cell. I talked to George about the idea. He spent six weekends in prison, while he continued to work throughout the week.

---

*The federal probation system is divided into "risk" categories. In the low-risk category, only 3 percent of the offenders had their probation status revoked; in the moderate-risk group, the number increased to 10 percent; and in the high-risk group, it was as high as 37 percent. However, a violation of probation did not necessarily mean that the offender was returned to prison; in most cases, they were sent back to court.

"That's a very strange experience. It is like living a double life. Free during the week and prisoner on the weekend," he said.

You can see that we do have some alternatives to prison. Perhaps we do not have enough. Many would argue that we have not tried some new and creative ideas. Certainly, the community-based approach, or the halfway house, is a cheaper as well as a far more humane way of handling punishment for committing some of the nonviolent crimes.

However, most experts would agree that unless we can make good and productive citizens out of the prisoners, they will continue to commit crimes as a way of survival as well as a way of life. If we don't help break that pattern, our prisons will continue to be overcrowded, the costs will continue to mount, and we'll have a vicious cycle of crime and expensive, nonrehabilitative punishment.

THE ROAD BACK

"What's your greatest fear?" I asked Rodney.

"Getting out, getting out of here." Rodney leaned back on his hard, institutional chair in a maximum-security prison. "I'll be leaving in a couple of months, and, I tell you, all I can do is pray. I don't ever want to come back here, but I can't tell you I never will."

"Why?" I asked.

"Because I have been locked up for three years, and I don't know what it's like to be out there anymore."

Rodney met with his parole board, the committee that decides, after the minimum sentence has been served, if an inmate is ready to be released from prison. He was released a few months later. He said that throughout the time he was in prison, he woke up with nightmares about getting out. Once he got out we stayed in touch. The road back was hard. When he came out, he had no place to stay, so he stayed with his sister. He and his sister had a fairly good relationship, but her own circumstances weren't very good either. She had two children and worked as a receptionist, trying to make ends meet. Her husband had been out of work for a few months.

Rodney had not expected to stay there for long—a few weeks, he thought, just until he found a job and an apartment. Rodney's first task was to get on welfare, so that he would have some money until he got a job.

"What kind of job are you planning to look for?"

"Anything."

While in prison, Rodney got his high school equivalency certificate. During his three years there, he did maintenance work around the prison, made license plates, and worked in the cafeteria. But he still did not have any specialized skills. He figured that he would try to get a job in the garment district, pushing carts of merchandise from the warehouse onto the delivery trucks bound for the department stores.

The first few weeks were a little strange for Rodney. Being on the outside was a new feeling. He stayed home a lot and watched television because he was afraid of his old friends and he had not made any new ones. He did see some relatives whom he had not talked with in years.

"When I was on the streets, I didn't go by my mother's house because I knew that she didn't want to see me high. So now that I got out I spent a lot of time with her and her lady friends. I even went to church with her. I can't tell you how happy I made her."

Of course, after a few weeks, Rodney got restless, staying with his sister and visiting his mother. He took a bus ride through his neighborhood where he used to commit crimes of burglary and robbery. He didn't get off the bus. In fact, looking out the window, seeing his friends on the street just "hanging out," he said to himself how useless their life must be. In the meantime, he tried to get a job in the garment district. After about three or four attempts, he gave up.

"Man, I don't even know how to get a job. I don't know what I'm doing wrong but I don't even get beyond filling out the forms."

"Do you put on the application that you have been arrested?" I asked.

"Of course, shouldn't I? I am trying to live an honest life."

After three weeks with no job, Rodney became very anxious. He knew that he should move out of his sister's apartment and find a room. After looking around, Rodney found a furnished hotel room that he could afford. That's not so easy to do in a place like New York, where rents are very high. The room was dingy, but Rodney had not planned to stay there for long, so he tried to get used to it. It was about as small as most people's bathrooms, and the roaches were ample, something that he was used to in prison. The hotel smelled bad and most of the other tenants were also on welfare. Some were elderly, some physically disabled, and a few were prostitutes.

"I figured that I would just use the place to stay for a short while so I could deal with it, but I tell you, it really got to me—the filth, the smell, plus that small room reminded me of prison. As time went on I met a few people there. One of the people that I got to know was a woman who worked out of that hotel. She prostituted herself to support her drug habit. Now, I knew that nothing was worse for me than to live with a 'dope fiend' woman, but then, who else would have me?"

As Rodney rationalized the incident, I realized how his hopes had faded. He still had no job, no money other than welfare checks, and a lot of time on his hands.

Rodney started hanging out at a bar in the same neighborhood. Within a month, he was using heroin again and got arrested for the sale of drugs. After he spent some time in jail awaiting trial, the charges were dismissed.

When Rodney was released from jail, we met again.

Rodney shook his head and said, "I can't tell you how easy it is to fall back into the same pattern. After the frustration of not getting a job, not knowing anyone but my family, I just couldn't deal with the whole situation.

"What are you going to do now?" I asked.

"This time I know that I can't do it alone. I am going to go to one of the organizations that work with prisoners. I am not even going to try to do it alone."

There are numerous agencies that work with ex-convicts. One of them, Fortune Society, located in New York City, has been in existence for about fifteen years, offering moral support and counseling, helping in job placement, and providing a place for ex-convicts to meet other people with prison records who are serious about staying out of prison.

David Rothenberg, Fortune's founder and president, said to me that when people ask him what's new about Fortune, he replies, "The next person coming in the door." All of Fortune Society's counselors are ex-convicts. They, too, have experienced the difficulties of readjusting to the outside world.

One of the counselors that I talked with at Fortune had been in and out of prison for twenty years before he decided to change his life, but once he made that decision, he never returned.

"All I can say is that I was ready. Until you are ready to give it up, there's nothing that anyone can do for you. You have to be ready to never go back, tired of being in prison."

I asked, "Is it just a matter of getting a job, and having an income and something to do?"

"No, it's a matter of first deciding that you don't ever want to go back to prison."

Of course, that's easier said than done. Interestingly, this man's experiences were similar to Rodney's, and yet he overcame them. Why? He said that, after twenty years in and out of prison, he decided he would do anything to stay free. He also came out of prison with no place to go, so he got a room in a run-down hotel, got a job in the garment district pushing carts packed with clothes, made about $120 a week, stayed in his hotel room, and watched television until he happened to hear about Fortune Society. He found friends there, a new outlook and direction, and, most of all, a place where people cared. From being a program participant, he became a staff member and now, as counselor, he says that he likes to give to others what has been given to him—guidance, support, help with getting a job, advice even on how to look for work.

"When some people come to us, they are literally starting over—starting from scratch. They have nothing."

I wondered why Rodney didn't make it and the counselor did. One thing for certain, it takes a tremendous determination, a lot of help, the ability to find work, or a place to belong, the ability to find a new community of friends and a way to keep from being lonely. That's not so easy.

In many ways, it's harder for the women, yet the rate of recidivism, or the number of them who return to prison, is lower than it is for men. According to most of the statistics, about 50 to 60 percent of the men and about 30 percent of the women return to prison. Many women are released from prison with not only the problems of not having a job, or money, or a place to stay, but have their children to worry about, something that most men don't even mention.

Sarah, who went through a halfway house for women, has been out of prison for over a year and has been able to make an excellent adjustment, but not without a lot of pain and frustration. Before Sarah was arrested, she had been a drug addict and spent her days committing robbery or snatching purses to support her heroin habit. She has two children. While she was in prison, her mother-in-law took care of them, bringing the children to see her occasionally. Sarah was considered a model prisoner. After she was released, she entered a halfway house. Even with a very strong and positive attitude, she found it very hard.

Eventually she did get a job, but she earns very little money. She lives in an area that is drug-infested and dangerous, so she doesn't want her children to live with her until she can find a safer place. She would like to go to college but she knows that it will take awhile before she'll have enough money. She reasons that with a degree she can make more money. In the meantime, every day after work she goes to see her children and eats dinner with them before returning home.

"I'm trying. I'm really trying," she said.

Aside from all the other problems, having a "record," a criminal record, is one of the hardest to overcome for someone coming out of prison. Several ex-convicts told me that they did not want to lie. They felt that they had spent their life lying, running from the police, running from people, and they did not want to feel that way on a job. But the fact that a lot of people do not want to hire someone out of prison makes it even more difficult for them. What some of them have done is lie to get the job, and, once they felt comfortable with their bosses, told the truth.

As one ex-convict said, "I told him because I felt secure with him, I was doing a good job, and I was there a year. My boss was surprised, but it made no difference to him by then. However, had I told him the truth in the beginning, I don't think that he would have hired me."

It's hard to say who will make it and who will be back in prison, but some things seem to be important. The level of family support really seems to make a difference. Of course, in Rodney's case, his family was there to support him and he still didn't seem to make the adjustment. Other important factors are education, a job, and the type of crime committed. When women commit manslaughter or murder, it tends to involve a family member, such as their child, their husband, or boyfriend. That type of crime is not usually committed again. They are crimes of passion, committed in a moment of anger or in a state of being drunk or high on drugs. Burglaries, robberies, and drug-related crimes are usually repeated. Compelled to support a drug habit by committing crimes daily, a person released from prison will most likely return unless he or she makes a commitment to get off drugs.

"It's a very hard road back, but it's not impossible," my friend at Fortune said. "No one can do this one for you. Your mother can't do it, no program can do it. They can help. But only you can decide that you are really tired of living in a zoo, being mistreated, locked in a cell like an animal. If you get tired enough, you will not do it. You'll decide that you'll never go back to prison. That is no place to be for any human being."

Like most major issues, the problems of crime, punishment, and prisoners have no easy solutions. There are many different opinions, many factors to consider, and many different answers are proposed, none of them necessarily the right answers or the only answers. Reading about Sandra, or Rodney, or a young offender like Henry, you had a chance to see some of the problems yourself.

Why should we care about these people at all? you may ask. Well, we have to care because they are a part of our society, whether we know someone in prison or not. They are very much with us, and we have to decide what to do about them.

Perhaps the most crucial question is how do we prevent people from choosing a way of life that leads to crime and eventually to prison? What can we, as a society, do to stop this ever-growing number of people who are going to spend their lives living off their victims while they live behind bars? Obviously, for our own good, we need to break this cycle, this vicious way of life that harms all of us.

INDEX